The Story of the Blackfoot People

Niitsitapiisinni

The Story of the Blackfoot People

Niitsitapiisinni

THE BLACKFOOT GALLERY COMMITTEE

FIREFLY BOOKS

A FIREFLY BOOK

Published by Firefly Books Ltd. 2013

The publisher gratefully acknowledges the financial support for our publishing program by the Government of Canada through the Canada Book Fund as administered by the Department of Canadian Heritage

First printing

Publisher Cataloging-in-Publication Data (U.S.)

The story of the Blackfoot people : Niitsitapiisinni / The Blackfoot Gallery Committee.
Originally published 2001.
[104] p. : ill. (some col.), maps ; cm.
Includes bibliographical references and index.
Summary: : In an innovative partnership with the Glenbow Museum in Calgary, Alberta, a team of elders and spiritual leaders from the Blackfoot community agreed to share their history, traditions and artifacts in an effort to document their lives.
ISBN-13: 978-1-77085-181-8 (pbk.)
1. Siksika Indians -- History. 2. Piegan Indians -- History. 3. Kainah Indians -- History. 4. Indians of North America – history. I. Glenbow Museum. Blackfoot Gallery Committee. II. Title.
978.004/9745 dc23   E99.S4S76 2013

Library and Archives Canada Cataloguing in Publication

The story of the Blackfoot people : Niitsitapiisinni / Blackfoot Gallery Committee.
Previous title: Nitsitapiisinni.
Includes bibliographical references and index.
ISBN 978-1-77085-181-8
1. Siksika Indians--History. I. Glenbow Museum. Blackfoot Gallery Committee II. Title: Niitsitapiisinni.
E99.S54S76 2013   971.004'97352   C2012-907583-3

Published in the United States by
Firefly Books (U.S.) Inc.
P.O. Box 1338, Ellicott Station
Buffalo, New York 14205

Published in Canada by
Firefly Books Ltd.
50 Staples Avenue, Unit 1
Richmond Hill, Ontario L4B 0A7

All maps and photos courtesy of the Glenbow Museum, Calgary, Alberta, except page 30 (bottom right) and page 95 (inset) courtesy of the Provincial Archives of Manitoba, Edmund Morris Collection. For more information please visit www.glenbow.org.

Cover and interior design:
Erin R. Holmes/Soplari Design

Cover Images:
The Glenbow Museum

Printed in China

Table of Contents

Acknowledgments

This book arose from the development of an exhibition which focused on the Blackfoot legacy. Both projects had their origin over a decade ago when I first began to meet with Blackfoot people and learn about their history and culture.

Bob Janes, President and CEO of Glenbow from 1989 to 1999, was always supportive of our initiatives of cooperation and collaboration. This support has continued with those who have followed him in this role. The interest shown by the Honourable Ralph Klein, Premier of Alberta, has been vital as has the support of Glenbow's Board of Governors and staff and the people of the Blackfoot communities.

Funding was vital to making the gallery and book a reality. We thank the Alberta 2005 Centennial Initiative, Calgary Community Lottery Board, Calgary Facilities Enhancement Programs, and Department of Canadian Heritage Museums Assistance Program. The New Sun Fund of the Calgary Foundation also generously contributed to this project as did several anonymous donors who share a long association with Glenbow and a keen Interest in our western heritage. We thank Shell Canada Limited, the exclusive corporate sponsor of the gallery, for its commitment to promoting a greater understanding of, and respect for Aboriginal people.

The Blackfoot Gallery Committee includes, as core members: Doreen Blackweasel (Amsskaapipiikuni); Tom Blackweasel (Amsskaapipiikuni); Andy Black Water (Kainai); Jenny Bruised Head (Kainai); Beth Carter (Glenbow); Gerry Conaty (Glenbow); Clifford Crane Bear (Siksika); Louise Crop Eared Wolf (Kainai); Charlie Crow Chief (Kainai); Anita Dammer (Glenbow); Rosie Day Rider (Kainai); Terry Gunvordahl (Glenbow); Irene Kerr (Glenbow); Earl Old Person (Amsskaapipiikuni); Allan Pard (Apatohsipiikuni); Jerry Potts (Apatohsipiikuni); Pat Provost (Apatohsipiikuni); Irvine Scalplock (Siksika); Pete Standing Alone (Kainai); Jim Swag (Apatohsipiikuni); Donna Weaselchild (Siksika); Frank Weasel Head (Kainai); Clarence Wolfleg (Siksika); Herman Yellow Old Woman (Siksika).

We also acknowledge the support of the many people at Glenbow and Firefly Books who ensured the success of this project.

Gerald Conaty
Director, Indigenous Studies, Glenbow

Introduction

A great deal has transpired in the decade following the initial publication of this book that coincided with the opening of the new Blackfoot gallery at Glenbow in 2001. In 2008, Prime Minister Stephen Harper issued a formal apology to former students of the Indian Residential Schools. This was followed by Canada's signing of the United Nations Declaration on the Rights of Indigenous People in 2010. Aboriginal people remain the fastest growing segment of Canada's population and the number of Native students graduating from post-secondary institutions continues to increase.

And yet, First Nations cultures and histories remain largely unknown to most non-Native Canadians. In addition, as more Aboriginal children grow up in urban settings, they may have weaker connections with their language and traditional culture. We are addressing these needs through a unique partnership with Blackfoot traditionalists that presents "our way of life" through a museum gallery, an educational website [www.glenbow.org/blackfoot] for children in English, French and Blackfoot and this publication. Glenbow staff contributed their own skills to the wisdom brought by the Blackfoot to achieve these incredible accomplishments. It is our sincere hope that, through these resources, we can help create an atmosphere of recognition and respect.

Donna Livingstone
Interim President and CEO, Glenbow Museum

Our ability to adapt to the environment and to change is infinite and assures our survival. The struggles Indian people went through to survive assimilation by the United States and Canadian governments have made us stronger and it is through this experience that we can conquer the obstacles ahead.

This book shares the relationships between the four bands of the Blackfoot and the territory they occupied. The stories we share provide the origins of our values, teachings, beliefs and spirituality. It is our story, in our words, as we know it to be. The relationship among the Blackfoot people will never end.

Earl Old Person
Chairman, Blackfeet Tribal Council

Chapter 1
Niitsitapiisinni
Our Way of Life

10

"This is a good opportunity to let the world know we are here and what we are about."

ALLAN PARD,
APATOHSIPIIKUNI

Oki. Hello.

We are the Blackfoot people and this is our story. It is the story of how our traditions and values were given to us by Creator and other Spirit Beings. It is the story of our place in the universe and our relationship with all of Creation. We have learned this story through our traditional teachings, which we wish to share with you.

Our story is also about our struggle to maintain our values, principles and beliefs in the face of relentless change. For centuries we were a strong, independent people. Then whisky and disease began to destroy us. The buffalo, the mainstay of our existence, disappeared from our land. The governments of Canada and the United States promised help. In return they forced us to live on reserves, to give up our ancient beliefs and to stop speaking our own language. The governments thought we would either die off or be assimilated.

We have survived. Much has changed in our culture, and many young people have difficulty learning our language. But the core values of our culture are still important to us. Our ceremonies continue to affirm our connection with all of the natural world.

We hope you will learn from this story and understand who we are. It is only through such understanding that all of us will be able to live together in this land.

Who We Are

We are commonly called Blackfoot, but we have various names for ourselves. We recognize three tribes: the *Kainai* (Many Leaders, also called the Blood); the *Piikuni* or Peigan (including the *Amsskaapipiikuni* in Montana and *Apatohsipiikuni* in southern Alberta); and the *Siksika* (Blackfoot, also called Northern Blackfoot). We share a common language and culture. We intermarried and fought to keep common enemies from our territory.

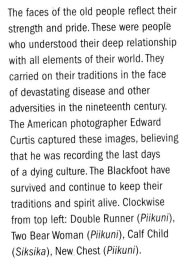

The faces of the old people reflect their strength and pride. These were people who understood their deep relationship with all elements of their world. They carried on their traditions in the face of devastating disease and other adversities in the nineteenth century. The American photographer Edward Curtis captured these images, believing that he was recording the last days of a dying culture. The Blackfoot have survived and continue to keep their traditions and spirit alive. Clockwise from top left: Double Runner (*Piikuni*), Two Bear Woman (*Piikuni*), Calf Child (*Siksika*), New Chest (*Piikuni*).

We have yet more names for ourselves. *Nii-tsi-ta-pii-ksi* means Real People and includes all of the indigenous peoples of North America. *Sao-kitapiiksi* is our name for the people who lived on the Plains. *Niitsi-poi-yksi* are the speakers of the Real Language — our language.

In the past we were not united in any alliance. However, because the three divisions often supported one another, many white people referred to us as the Blackfoot Confederacy. Today we have developed a formal political

The Rocky Mountains mark the western boundary of traditional Blackfoot territory. The Livingstone Range rises above the prairies as a solid wall, appearing much like the liners inside a tipi. The Blackfoot call these the "tipi liners." Atmospheric conditions can make this range appear close or farther away. Hence, the "tipi liners" can be used to predict the weather.

alliance to address common grievances with the Canadian and United States governments and to find ways of keeping our culture alive.

Our Traditional Territory

Niitawahsi is our name for our territory. Our ancient stories tell us that we were given this territory by *Ihtsi-pai-tapi-yopa*, our Creator and Essence of Life. These stories assert our right to exist here.

Our traditional territory extended from *Ponoka-si-sahta* (Elk River, the North Saskatchewan River) south to *Otahkoi-tah-tayi* (the Yellowstone River). We lived along the eastern slopes of the Rocky Mountains and eastward beyond *Omahski-spatsi-koyii* (the Great Sand Hills in what is now Saskatchewan). It is an immense land, with some of the richest natural resources in the world.

We knew every detail of this land. Our people traveled constantly throughout it, and their trails were well marked across the grasslands. They lived by hunting game

Blackfoot traditional territory.

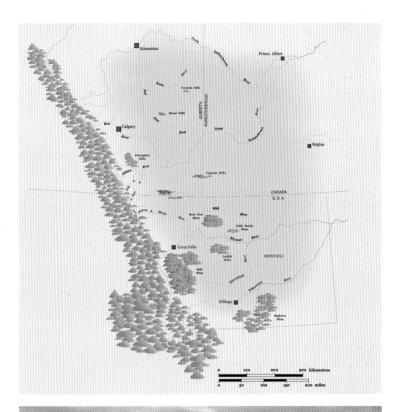

and collecting plants. By moving camp frequently, they were able to avoid depleting the resources in any one area. Our people knew the places where different plants grew and where game was plentiful. Their lives were nomadic, but their movements were not aimless: they always traveled with a purpose.

Another reason our people moved throughout their territory was to prevent their neighbors from encroaching on our lands. Our people believed that this territory and all the resources in it had been given to them to use. Other First Nations people were welcome to visit and trade, but not to take our game.

Ponoka-si-sahta (literally, Elk River), the North Saskatchewan River, marks the northern limit of the Blackfoot territory. The aspen parkland of this region is in marked contrast to the open grasslands farther south. It was an environment rich in beavers, and the fur traders used this river as a route into the Blackfoot homeland.

The broken badlands of the Milk River valley are a special place to the Blackfoot. Here they recorded their history and ancient stories in pictures carved into the stone. Other images were placed there by Spirit Beings to remind the Blackfoot of their traditions and to tell of future events.

14

Along the modern-day border of Saskatchewan and Alberta lie *Omahski-spatsi-koyii*, the Great Sand Hills. This expanse of dunes is home to countless deer and pronghorn antelope. It is also the place to which Blackfoot spirits go after death. It is a place to be avoided by all living people.

Over the centuries the different groups among our people developed the habit of living in different parts of our territory. The *Siksika* were usually found along the northern and eastern part of the territory, the *Kainai* lived in the central part, while the *Piikuni* camped along the foothills in the west.

Chapter 2

The Blackfoot World

(PREVIOUS PAGE) Sweet Pine Hills, Montana; tipi pegs (inset).

One of our ancient stories tells of the time *Napi* gave his buffalo robe to a big rock and then took it back again. No animal could stop this rock as it chased *Napi*. Finally, two small birds dived at the rock and burst it to pieces. The big rock near the town of Okotoks, Alberta, is part of the rock that chased *Napi*. The rest of the debris is scattered southward along the foothills of Alberta and Montana. The name Okotoks comes from the Blackfoot word *Ohkohtok*, which means rock.

In order to understand who we are, it is first necessary to understand the world around us. Our perceptions influence how we interact with other people and with other elements of our environment. We do not separate our beliefs from other parts of our life. Our spirituality and beliefs permeate our entire existence.

Ihtsi-pai-tapi-yopa is the name we give to the Essence of All Life. This is Creator, the Source of All Life. *Ihtsi-pai-tapi-yopa* made all living things equal; humans were not given the right to rule over or exploit the rest of nature. We recognize plants, animals and rocks as other living beings, who are different from us but also our equals.

Each plant and animal has unique gifts and abilities, which they share with humans. Some plants can cure our diseases; others give us important nutrients. Bison are strong animals who provided much of what we needed for survival. Birds are swift flyers who helped warriors to be stealthy and quick. These animals visited us in human form and taught us how to call on them for their special gifts. This is how we became so closely connected to all the beings with whom we share the earth.

We use the word *Nii-tsi-ta-pii-ksi* to refer to ourselves and to all other First Nations people. This means "Real People" and distinguishes us as human beings from the rest of Creation.

The other beings who live around us inhabit different environments. We share the earth with four-legged animals, plants, rocks and the earth itself. We call these *ksahkomi-tapii-ksi* (Earth Beings). The *Spomi-tapii-ksi* (Above Beings) live in the sky. Among these are *Natosi* (the Sun), his wife *Kokomi-kisomm* (the Moon) and their son *Ipisowahsi* (the Morning Star). Other stars, thunder, the sky and many birds are also *spomi-tapii-ksi*.

In and near the water live the water birds, beaver, otter and muskrat. These have often helped our people by showing us how to use their powers. Other water beings, such as horned snakes, are dangerous and try to take us into the water with them. This is why we offer food or tobacco to the water spirits whenever we cross a river or lake. Our word for these water beings is *soyii-tapii-ksi*.

At one time Blackfoot men and women lived apart. While the women wore finely tanned hides and had plenty to eat, the men dressed in roughly tanned hides and were starving. *Napi* brought the men to where the women were camped, at a place now called Women's Buffalo Jump. The men and women each chose a partner. However, when the leader of the women did not choose *Napi*, he became angry and changed himself into a tree.

"When we pray, we call upon the sun, the moon, the stars, the Milky Way, the earth and everything in it."

LOUISE CROP EARED WOLF,
KAINAI

Blackfoot practices are often rooted in ancient stories. For example, they say that once, when *Napi* was being blown about by a strong wind, he grasped a black birch. The tree bent but did not break, enabling *Napi* to resist the buffeting gale. To this day the Blackfoot make their tipi pegs from black birch. They believe that just as this tree helped *Napi*, it will also keep Blackfoot tipis from blowing down.

Another story tells of the dangerous thorns on bull berry bushes. *Napi* got around this problem by waiting until the first frost and beating the branches with a stick so that the fruit fell into a hide bucket. This is still how the Blackfoot collect bull berries.

How Our Traditions Were Given to Us

Our ancient stories tell us how our traditions were given to us. These teachings show us how to live and explain our relationship with the other beings in Creation. For us, these stories are true. They are the record of our history since the beginning of time.

The following are short versions of some of these stories. These examples illustrate our close connection with all of Creation. Each of the stories happened at a specific place in our traditional territory.

Napi: Old Man

Napi, Old Man, always acted on impulse. He was rude, mean and stingy. He often lied and played dirty tricks. He was always getting into trouble and suffering the consequences of his bad behavior. And yet, he did not act out of malice. He merely overdid things and caused chaos as a result.

One of our basic principles is to live a balanced life, and our stories about *Napi* teach us the importance of this. *Napi* went to extremes and failed to maintain a balance.

Napi's adventures also teach us about our environment. We learn why wolf willow (or silverberry) smells bad when it is burned. We learn why we use black birch for tipi pegs. We learn why we collect bull berries only after the first frost and by beating the bush rather than by picking the berries.

Napi's impulsive behavior left our world all mixed up. There was no order. It was a wild and dangerous place for our ancestors.

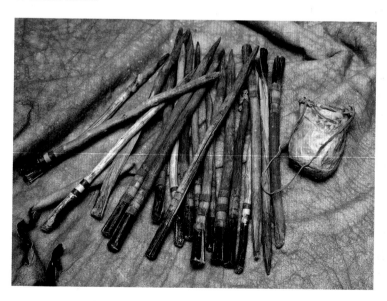

Katoyissa: Blood Clot

An old couple camped with their son-in-law, who was married to three of their daughters. The son-in-law was very cruel. He made his father-in-law chase buffalo for him but did not share the food with the old couple. Only the youngest daughter pitied them and took food to their tipi.

One day the old man found a clot of blood on the prairie. He hid it from his son-in-law and took it to his wife, telling her to cook it in a soup. As the water boiled, the old couple heard a baby crying. Looking into the pot, they saw a child, who instructed them to take him out and hold him up to each pole in the tipi. As the old couple did so, the child grew and became a young man named *Katoyissa*, or Blood Clot. After hearing the old people's story, *Katoyissa* devised a plan to kill the son-in-law and the daughters who did not help their parents.

Once he had saved the old couple, *Katoyissa* traveled throughout our territory, saving our people from various evil beings who kept them captive. He killed the Bears, Big-Snake Man, the Blood Suckers, the Inhaler and others. When *Katoyissa* was finished, our people were free to travel throughout the territory *Ihtsi-pai-tapi-yopa* had given them. The world was now safe for our people.

We believe that *Katoyissa* now sleeps at the place called the Sweet Grass Hills (although we call them *Katoyissiksi*, the Sweet Pine Hills).

Makoi-yohsokoyi: The Wolf Trail

Makoiyi, the wolves, were the first Earth Beings to pity us. One winter, when our people were starving, a young man and his family camped by themselves as they searched for food. The wolves found the family and appeared to them as young men bringing fresh meat to the tipi. The wolves took this family with them, showing the man how to cooperate with other people when he hunted buffalo and other

"All of our being is connected, spiritually and physically, to our homelands."

ANDY BLACK WATER, *KAINAI*

19

animals. The wolves told our ancestors that animals with hoofs and horns were all right to eat, but that animals with paws and claws should be left alone.

The wolves disappeared in the spring, but we still see them in the sky as *makoi-yohsokoyi*, the Wolf Trail (the Milky Way). These stars constantly remind us of how we should live together.

Sacred Bundles

Katoyissa made the world safe. *Makoiyi* taught our people the value of living and working together. Still, our people starved and suffered. They did not know how to ask the other beings for help.

Through the ages the *naa-to-yi-ta-piiksi*, or Spirit Beings, took pity on our ancestors and came to help them.

> "All the songs and ceremonies came from the other side, from the spirit world, animal world."
>
> ANDY BLACK WATER, *KAINAI*

Naa-to-yi-ta-piiksi changed themselves into human form and taught our ancestors the ceremonies and songs that we could use to call on them for help. *Naa-to-yi-ta-piiksi* also gave our ancestors physical objects that are now kept together in sacred bundles. These bundles are our connection to *naa-to-yi-ta-piiksi*, and we use them in our ceremonies.

Naa-to-yi-ta-piiksi continue to live among us and help us in our lives. We must always be mindful of this and respect their presence. In this way our understanding of the world is very different from that of non-Native people.

There are many, many stories about our sacred bundles. What follows is just a small sample. They will show you how some of our traditions were given to us.

Sacred bundles contain items that were given to the Blackfoot by the Spirit Beings of their world. These are used in ceremonies to renew the connections with the Spirit Beings and Creator and to ask for help. When not in use, these bundles were carefully hung along the west wall of the tipis, above the inhabitants as they sat or slept. Today they are kept in quiet rooms in people's homes and are accorded the care one would give to a child.

Iinisskimm: Buffalo Calling Stones

Although our people began to live as *makoiyi* had shown them, life was still very hard and the people were often hungry. One day *Iiniiksi* (buffalo) took pity on our people. A lady named Weasel Woman was collecting water from a river near her camp when she heard something calling to her from the bushes. When she looked closer, she found a stone that spoke to her. The stone explained how it could be used in a ceremony that would call the buffalo towards a *pis-skaan* (buffalo jump).

Weasel Woman took the *iinisskimm*, the buffalo calling stone, back to camp. She told the spiritual leaders about the ceremony to call the buffalo. The people followed her instructions and soon they had plenty of meat and many hides for new tipi covers.

There are numerous *iinisskimm* on the prairies. Many people still keep them as sacred bundles. We call on *iinisskimm* to help us have successful lives.

Ksisk-staki: Beaver

There was a poor man whom people called Scabby-Round-Robe after the poorly tanned hides he wore for clothes. Scabby-Round-Robe wished to marry a wealthy woman, and he was greatly saddened by her low regard for him.

One day he wandered away from camp to the edge of a lake. There, as he slept, a boy appeared and took Scabby-Round-Robe to his father. This boy and his father were *ksisk-staki* (beavers). They kept Scabby-Round-Robe with them all winter. The Old Man Beaver gave Scabby-Round-Robe many powers.

In the spring, Scabby-Round-Robe returned to his people and used his new powers to become a successful warrior. He married the woman and was given many sacred things by other men in camp, which he kept together in the Beaver Bundle.

We continue to keep Beaver Bundles. When we open them, we call on the animals to help us be successful and happy.

The beavers who helped Scabby-Round-Robe lived in a lake near what is now Waterton Lakes National Park in southern Alberta.

Ponoka: Elk

An elk's wife was taken away by another bull elk. The husband looked everywhere for her, and he asked moose and crow to help.

When at last he found his wife and the other bull, the husband threatened them by charging a pine tree. The other bull retaliated, knocking the tree down. The husband, moose and crow were frightened and ran away.

After a while they returned and offered gifts to the bull elk. Crow gave his feathers; Elk gave his antlers. The bull elk returned the wife to her husband.

Later, the bull elk who had stolen the wife met a man who cared for a Beaver Bundle. The bull elk changed himself into a young man and gave the crow feathers and elk antlers to the Beaver Bundle owner. Today, the antlers appear as the headdress worn by the Holy Woman at our *ookaan* (sun dance), while the crow feathers are worn by her male partner.

These events took place near the present-day town of High River, Alberta, which is called *Spiitsii* in Blackfoot.

Ksiistsi-komm: Thunder

Ksiistsi-komm (Thunder) was jealous of a man and wanted his wife. He struck their tipi, knocked them unconscious and stole the woman. When the man recovered, he wandered all over, asking many animals to help him find his wife. All were afraid of the power of Thunder. Finally, *Omahkai-stow* (Raven) agreed to help.

23

He flew to Thunder's home and challenged him.

  Ksiistsi-komm shot lightning bolts at *Omahkai-stow*, trying to kill him. But *Omahkai-stow* used his own power and, by flapping his wings, brought on the cold north wind and snow. Gradually, the cold slowed down *Ksiistsi-komm* until he could no longer send out the dangerous bolts of lightning. It was a long battle, but eventually *Ksiistsi-komm* gave up and returned the man's wife.

  Omahkai-stow insisted that he and *Ksiistsi-komm* divide the year into two parts: winter, which is *Omahkai-*

stow's season, and summer, which is *Ksiistsi-komm*'s time.

Omahkai-stow also ordered *Ksiistsi-komm* to make a peace treaty with the man and to give our people his pipe as a sign of this agreement. From that day onward we have opened our Thunder Medicine Pipe Bundles each spring at the first sound of thunder. We ask for good weather, good crops and good luck for the coming year.

Omahkai-stow lived at the place now called Crowsnest Mountain. *Ksiistsi-komm* lived at Ninastako, or Chief Mountain.

The design on Blackfoot painted tipis are not merely decorative. Often, Spirit Beings gave these images to people in their dreams so that prosperity, harmony and long lives would come to those inside the tipi. These designs describe, among other things, the origin story and the recollections of people who have been helped by the design. The right to paint a design is transferred from one individual to another in a formal, public ritual. Left to right, Antelope tipi, *Kainai*; Bear tipi, *Siksika*; Star tipi, *Kainai*; Horned Snake tipi, *Piikuni*.

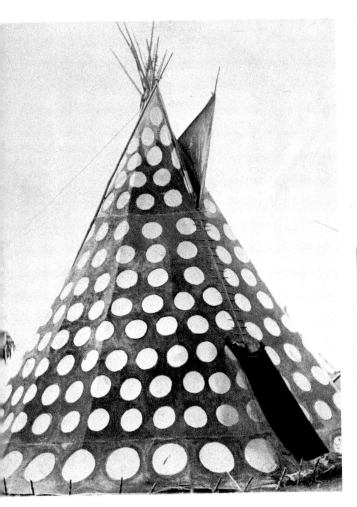

Niitoy-yiss: **Painted Tipis**

The designs that are painted on our tipis are more than pretty images; they connect us with the other beings in the world around us. These painted tipis are another of our sacred bundles. The right to use any of the designs is a privilege and must be transferred in a ceremony. Not all of our tipis are painted.

Accompanying the designs are ceremonies for specific purposes. Some help us to predict the future, some to call the buffalo, others to call a storm. Each design protects the family inside and helps them to live happy, successful and safe lives.

Each part of this Otter design tipi has a special significance. The circles on the ear flaps are stars, representing the Big Dipper (seven circles) and the "bunch stars" (*Pleiades*; six circles). Stories about these stars tell of children who were lost or neglected and went to live in the sky. The cross on the back is a butterfly or moth, who represents the Dream Beings and calls on them to bring good dreams to the people inside. Below the cross is a circle for Morning Star. The design on the bottom represents the foothills where this design was given to human beings. The animal around the middle is an otter, who has given the people access to his powers to help them in their lives.

Chapter 3

How We Lived Together

(Previous Page) *Piikuni* camp, Montana; *Siksika* shirt (inset).

A long time ago the wolves took pity on our people and taught them to live together as wolves do.

Wolves live in packs, with a mature female and male in charge. Together, the pack hunts for food and raises its young. Juvenile members often leave the pack when they are old enough to mate.

Our people lived together in clans. Children, parents, aunts, uncles and grandparents lived and traveled together. As a rule, when a woman married, she moved to her husband's camp. Any person who did not get along with his or her relations was free to move to another clan's camp. People were welcome in camp as long as they cooperated and respected other people.

It was part of our tradition that every summer all the clans would come together in a large circle camp called the *ako-katssinn*. Each clan had a special place within the circle; it never changed. Today each clan still has the same place in the circle. People never camp away from their clan's place.

One Gun was both a leader of traditional ceremonies and a politician. He emerged as an influential individual in the early years of the twentieth century and continued in public life through the 1960s. His role as a ceremonial leader kept many traditions alive in the face of government repression.

Leadership

In any group, certain individuals emerge as leaders. Personality, experience, judgment, speaking skills and generosity are all leadership qualities. In our clan camps, people with these qualities were acknowledged as leaders. They were careful to listen to everyone's advice, opinions, and experience. The advice and wisdom of our old people was especially important, and we placed much value on their life experiences. A wise leader sought their counsel and listened carefully to what they said. The knowledge and spiritual support of people who cared for the sacred bundles was always important too, as these people had an especially close tie to the *Naa-to-yi-ta-piiksi* and could ask for their support and help. A leader's decision had to reflect the consensus of the clan.

We recognize that each person has unique skills and experience, so our people acknowledged different leaders in different situations. A man who was a good buffalo

Rides-At-The-Door was widely known and respected for his traditional knowledge, kind disposition and generous nature. He presided over many types of ceremonies and, like One Gun, helped keep these traditions alive during repressive times. His door was always open to travelers who needed a meal or a place to stay. His judgment was valued whenever important decisions needed to be made.

Mrs. Margaret Bad Boy was born at Siksika late in the nineteenth century. Although she had no offspring of her own, she brought countless children into her home. As a member of many sacred societies, Mrs. Bad Boy knew the Blackfoot traditions and history and taught them to anyone who was willing to learn. She was an invaluable resource in *Siksika* land claim research.

hunter may not have been the best person to lead a raid against a neighbor.

Clan leadership was not inherited, but children did learn behavior and values from their adult relatives. As a result, leadership tended to stay within particular families, and sometimes an aging leader would publicly identify a relative to replace him.

"In the olden days, to become a Chief, he didn't say anything — people noticed him for what he did. You have to live it before you are recognized. You have to practice leadership qualities. First you have to be a warrior, a provider, generous. The overall Chief is recognized by all the clans — that is the way a person becomes Chief."

PETE STANDING ALONE,
KAINAI

Brings-Down-The-Sun was a widely respected spiritual leader and clan head. He was leader of the *Apatohsipiikuni* in the late 1800s, guiding them through the difficult transition to life on the Reserve.

Living in Camp

We always pitched our tipis with the doors facing east. Each morning our people opened the doors of their lodges so that their prayers could travel to the rising sun, helping *Natosi* reach above the horizon for another day. The tipis were not arranged in any particular order in our everyday camps, although close relations would be near each other.

Blackfoot camps usually comprised members of an extended family and other people who may have joined the clan. Tipi arrangements were not strictly defined, although all were erected facing east. It is said that this allowed morning prayers to travel towards the rising sun, helping it to come above the horizon for another day.

31

Sacred bundles are regarded as living beings, which must be cared for as one cares for a child. In the old days these bundles were taken outside each day and hung from tripods. As the sun moved across the sky, the bundles were moved around the tipi to ensure that they always faced *Natosi*. People avoided these bundles out of respect and endeavored to be quiet whenever they were near.

Our people spent most of their time outdoors. Tipis were mainly used for sleeping, to provide shelter from storms and as places for holding special meetings.

Each person was expected to contribute to the welfare of the camp as best they could. If people failed in these duties, the entire camp went without food, clothing or shelter. If people neglected their responsibilities, they did not survive. This responsibility to be a good provider continues to this day.

Our Men and Women Lived and Worked Together

Our ancient stories tell us that men and women had different, yet complementary, roles in our society. Our men and women had great respect for each other and for the differences in their roles. They knew and understood how much they needed each other to survive.

Men's Roles

Our men were often away from camp — hunting, protecting the territory, or scouting for strangers who might steal our women and children. It was a dangerous responsibility. To avoid danger and be successful hunters, our men needed to be fully aware of their environment and integrated with everything around them.

"Being generous, it is an important aspect of our life and teachings, to share the good fortunes with the rest."

ANDY BLACK WATER,
KAINAI

Men were the most mobile members of society. As hunters, they followed the migratory buffalo and elusive deer and elk. As protectors, they continually patrolled the areas surrounding the camps. Status and recognition came quickly to those who were the best hunters and bravest warriors. Death too could come quickly.

33

Women's Roles

Our women's roles were focused on the camp. Women were the foundation of the family, nurturing the children. They also cared for our sacred bundles, which we regard as living beings. Our women's skill at making "dry meat" and *moki-maani* (pemmican), and at tanning hides and sewing clothes and tipi covers kept us fed, clothed and sheltered. Many women were herbal healers as well, caring for the wellness of our people.

Food for Survival

Meat brought to camp was cured as quickly as possible and prepared for cooking and preserving. Choice cuts were roasted or boiled and eaten immediately.

The primary way of preserving meat was to slice it into thin strips that were then draped over poles. The sun quickly dried these fillets and the wind kept the flies away. This meat was stored for several weeks. In the fall the women ground this "dry meat" together with crushed berries and fat, using a stone maul lashed to a willow handle as a mallet, and a flat rock as a grinding stone. This mixture could be kept all winter and was often invaluable in times of starvation.

34

Our people cut meat into thin strips, which were hung to dry in the sun. Sometimes they made a fire with willow to remove any disease from the meat. They also put sage in the fire to keep away the flies. The dry meat was stored, with dry mint, in rawhide containers called *sootsi-maan*. The dried wild mint was used to keep insects away.

Bones were boiled in pits lined with buffalo stomachs. Grease from the bones rose to the surface and was skimmed off. After the Europeans brought copper and iron kettles, we boiled our food and bones in these new pots.

Our people dried berries in the sun and combined them with the dry meat, crushing the mixture with a heavy stone mallet. Fat was then added, creating *moki-maani*. Often, a good supply of *moki-maani* kept our people from starving during the cold winter.

Hides for Survival

Preparing hides was a very skilled task, and one that brought esteem to women who were talented at it. Children were often recruited to help, and knowledge of the process was passed down from generation to generation. Although the work was hard, it was also a social occasion, as the women worked in groups.

Tanning bison hides is arduous work. To remove the hair, the hide is staked on the ground and a scraper with an elk-antler handle and a stone or iron bit is drawn across the surface. When all of the hair has been taken off, the hide is turned over and the fat and cuticle is removed with a serrated metal or bone scraper. Brains and water are then rubbed on both surfaces to preserve the leather. Finally, the hide is drawn across a wire or rawhide rasp until the desired amount of pliability is achieved.

Tanning hides was key for survival. Shelter, clothes and containers all required well-tanned hides. The process was very time-consuming and demanding. Fresh hides needed to be processed quickly, before they spoiled.

In our ancient stories, *Ipisowahsi* (the Morning Star) came to us dressed in white hides. We continue to tan our hides white to remind us of our close relationship with *Ipisowahsi* and his father, *Natosi* (the Sun).

Sewing and Painting

Sewing beautiful clothes and painting hide containers required great skill, and our women took pride in their talent and artistry. Bone awls and sinew were their needle and thread. Our women proudly wore their awls in cases hung from their belts.

Paint and porcupine quills are our oldest ways of decorating clothes. Our people also traded with their neighbors for dentalium and cowrie shells, which they used as ornaments. Quill working was a very special skill, and

A hide shirt signaled the respected status of the man who wore it and reflected the skill of the woman who made it. The porcupine quillwork on this *Siksika* shirt is similar to a motif that seems to have originated among the *Mandan-Hidatsa-Arikara* people of the middle Missouri River area. The rosette on the chest and the scalp locks allude to the story of Scarface and the gifts that *Natosi* gave him to take to the Blackfoot people. The painted circles on the chest area reflect the owner's relationship to Thunder; perhaps he was keeper of a Thunder Medicine Pipe Bundle. Flicker feathers are also attached and have a special meaning known only to the original owner.

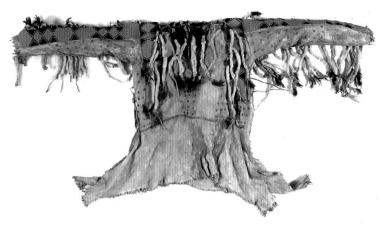

This shirt displays design elements similar to the previous one. The beaded strips, which replace the quillwork, are a distinctively Blackfoot design. Once again, painted circles draw a connection to the power of Thunder. Weasel (ermine) tails replace the hair locks but make the same link to the Scarface story. Weasels are considered powerful because of their ability to change color with the seasons. The triangular design at the neck is a Blackfoot design element, perhaps reflecting the way Blackfoot ceremonial leaders paint the altar before certain ceremonies.

we considered it to be sacred work. Before learning to quill a woman was transferred the rights to do this work by an older, experienced woman who also gave instructions as to the special protocols that needed to be followed. These precautions prevented injury from the sharp quills and kept the workers from damaging their eyes while doing such detailed work.

After the Europeans arrived, our people began trading for glass beads, ribbons, cloth and metal ornaments, which were brighter, more colorful and easier to work.

Women's dresses too reflected the status of the wearer. The painted yellow yoke, the blue-and-red triangle in the lower center, and the blue-edged red squares along the hem establish the owner of this elk-hide dress as a spiritual leader of her people. The wavy bands of beads across the bodice are a distinctively Blackfoot motif.

We Raised Our Children Together

The birth of a child is a wonderful event. In the days when we camped together in clans, newborns were cared for by all the women. Often, grandparents would adopt and raise a grandchild. From the first day of life we offered songs and prayers for a long and healthy life. After a few months we approached a respected adult to name the child. This name reflected achievements of the adult and brought blessings and success to the child. We still name our children in this way.

Our people watched with care and patience as their children grew. A child's natural abilities were allowed to blossom without interference. We had no grades or achievement tests. People developed according to their own abilities. Those with developmental problems were fully integrated in our society, participating with everyone else.

When children misbehaved, they were disciplined by their aunts and uncles. Usually, the child was spoken to privately and the importance of good behavior was explained.

"I grew up in a world of stories. They were told in winter. Small boys showed their respect to sit and listen to the stories and learn them and remember them for the future. The stories were very elaborate with lots of descriptive detail."

CLIFFORD CRANE BEAR, *SIKSIKA*

In the old days, everybody in the camp helped raise the children. Grandparents spent many hours telling stories to the young ones; this was how Blackfoot values were instilled in children. Older children watched over younger ones, keeping them from danger. Aunts and uncles were responsible for disciplining those who broke protocol. Parents showed their offspring basic life skills and were pillars of support. Two *Piikuni* girls (left); *Siksika* woman and child (right).

Often, one child would emerge as the favorite child or grandchild. This individual was spared from doing chores and shielded from the give-and-take of normal childhood interaction. If the family was wealthy, this *minipoka* received lavish gifts of elaborate buckskin clothing, horses and other material goods. Sometimes sacred bundles were transferred to them at a very young age. Miniature tipis were made and painted with sacred designs. Although some of these individuals grew to be successful leaders, others never acquired the proper acumen.

Teaching Our Values

Putting our values into practice was essential to survival. They were our principles for living together and for existing with all of Creation. Although all adults taught these values by example in everyday life, our ancient stories gave explicit expression to these messages. Usually, our old people were the ones who told these stories. While the nighttime was an important time for storytelling, grandparents might tell these stories any time. They constantly reinforced good behavior and provided advice through storytelling.

These stories are important throughout our lives, and their lessons change as we grow older. Often, when we ask older people for advice, they will tell us one of our ancient stories to put the issue in a bigger context. This offers us direction without giving specific instructions. Each person must find his or her path; an adviser can only offer general suggestions by means of stories.

"Respect is what links all the ideas together. Thankfulness to the Creator each morning and evening — to all the animals, birds, clans, earth, human life, nature."

JENNY BRUISED HEAD,
KAINAI

Learning through Play

Our children's toys were made from the materials at hand. The games children played helped them acquire the skills they would need in adult life. Toys were often made with the help of grandparents and were another link between the generations.

Twigs and sticks became horses and riders. A bent wire could be a racehorse and jockey, with colored yarn for the rider's silks. Knuckle and wrist bones from buffalo became horses. Boiled hoofs and scraps of hide, stuffed with grass or animal hair, were dolls. Flowered cotton scraps were used for doll pillows and mattresses.

Favored children sometimes had entire miniature camps made for them. Everything was to scale, including painted tipis, furniture and clothes.

Toys were generally made from whatever material was at hand. Sometimes, however, more effort was put into creating playthings. Tipis were cut from scraps of hide, as were dolls that were stuffed with grass, buffalo wool or anything that was nearby. The beading on these dolls' clothes may have been a girl's early effort at learning this skill.

42

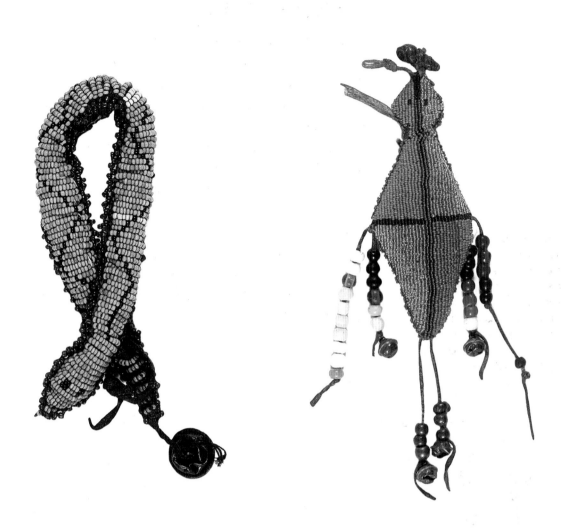

We call these children *minipoka*, or favored children. Their parents were usually wealthy, and toys were lavished on the children as a display of this wealth.

As children grew up, adult responsibilities replaced play. Boys and girls stopped playing together and began working with the older people.

The spiritual protection of the young has always been very important. Umbilical cords were saved and sewn into special pouches. These were worn by the child and kept his or her spirit nearby. The snake design was for boys, the lizard for girls. Since the colors and beadwork design were unique for each child, these amulets also made it easy for parents to identify their children from a distance.

Ookaan

Everything in our world is sacred. Each day we acknowledge *Ihtsi-pai-tapi-yopa* and all the *Naa-to-yi-ta-piiksi* in our world. Each year all of our clans come together to renew our connections with our universe. We call this the *ako-katssinn*, "the time of all people camping together."

At the center of an *ako-katssinn* is the ceremony we call *ookaan*. This focuses on a virtuous woman who has vowed to be the Holy Woman. For four days and nights she and her partner fast and pray in their tipi, which is set up in the center of the camp circle. They cut and dry one hundred buffalo tongues as an offering to bring a bountiful life to the people. When the couple break their fast, we erect a large, circular arbor near their tipi and raise a center pole within the structure. We put offerings of cloth on this pole so that *Natosi* will hear our prayers and give us a good year.

44

Once each year the *Amsskaapipiikuni*, *Apatohsipiikuni*, *Kainai* and *Siksika* gather for their *ookaan*. This ceremony renews the people's connection to *Natosi*, the sun and giver of life. As the people all camp together, this is also a time when the sacred societies undertake their ceremonies. Over the course of two or three weeks, ceremonies are performed that re-establish the Blackfoot people's relationship with all of Creation and reassert their right to live here. Bringing in willows for the sweat lodge (top); *Piikuni* encampment (bottom).

Social Dances

Our lives did not consist entirely of hard work and
ceremonies. Like all people, we enjoy socializing with our
friends and relations. Dances, hand games and horse races
were opportunities to laugh and joke with one another.
Sometimes these would be small gatherings at someone's
house. Other times, many people would come to a local
community hall. The *ako-katssinn* was always a time for
dancing in between the ceremonies.

The owl dance, the round dance and the snake
dance brought everyone into the dance circle. No one wore
special outfits; everyone just joined in.

Chicken Dancers and Grass Dancers, on the other
hand, wore special outfits that were unique to those dances.
Variations within the basic style were an expression of a
dancer's individuality.

The formal social dances often took
place at Christmas and other holidays
recognized by the mainstream society.
As this *Siksika* platform party indicates,
these events were usually sponsored
by the band council with the approval
of the Indian agent. It was a way to
bring people together and maintain
cohesiveness in the community.

45

Dancing has always been an important aspect of socializing. People often hosted informal round dances, owl dances and snake dances in their homes. On more formal occasions, when people gathered in community halls, there was a mixture of modern dress and traditional dance outfits. These were an opportunity for the Blackfoot to remember their past and preserve traditions that were otherwise being suppressed. *Siksika* Christmas dance, 1947 (left); *Siksika* dance, 1930s (right).

Hand games and horse races often involved gambling. They also taught our young men the skills of good hunters and warriors. Hand games trained people to concentrate and observe, while horse races required superb equestrian skills.

In a hand game, two teams sit facing one another with ten counting sticks. One side appoints someone to hide a pair of bones in one of his hands. The team then begins to beat on hand drums or tipi poles and sing while the hider sways and moves her hands about, trying to distract the guesser. With each successful guess a team collects one counting stick from the opposition. The game is over when a team collects all of the counting sticks.

Powwow

Today, most of our social dancing is done at powwows. At these large gatherings, there are dance and drumming competitions, which often carry a lot of prize money.

Powwows are important events where we can celebrate being Native without the prejudices of non-Native society. We make friends and form close relationships with people from all across North America. We exchange songs and dance styles with First Nations cultures from all over the continent.

Our powwows are open to everyone. We hope you will come, feel welcome and meet us.

Styles of dance outfits varied among the Native peoples of western North America. In the Chicken Dance, which is characteristic of the Blackfoot, the dancers imitate the movements of prairie chickens in their mating display. With quick steps the feather bustle vibrates rapidly and the large dance bells on the legs jingle. The porcupine and deer-hair roach on the dancer's head bobs, creating the illusion of even more frenzied movement.

47

People painted their faces for many different reasons. They usually used ocher, a mineral that was pulverized to a fine powder. This was mixed with rendered fat, which made the paint adhere to a person's skin. The fat and paint protected the skin from the sun and from the drying wind. Special patterns brought blessings and the protection of sacred bundles. Often, people were painted every day, but nowadays people usually have their faces painted only on special occasions. Double Steel and Two Cutter (previous page); Big Bull (top). Painting by Weinhold Reiss.

Everything the Blackfoot did had a special significance. For example, women (left) wore their hair in two braids to reflect their modesty. Men were more showy. Young boys often had three braids, symbolizing *Piikuni*, *Siksika* and *Kainai*. Sometimes men wore these braids all their lives. In some families all the men adopted the same hairstyle (center). The front topknot indicated that a man kept a Thunder Medicine Pipe Bundle (right).

49

Traditionally, the Blackfoot eagle-feather headdress was a distinctive circular crown of upright feathers. Horsehair was sometimes attached to the ends of the feathers and weasel tails hung from the brow band. A trailer of eagle feathers could augment the main bonnet. These headdresses carried spiritual blessings with them and were considered to be sacred bundles. A ceremonial transfer was required when a headdress passed from one person to another.

50

Chapter 4
Niitawahsin-nanni
The Place Where We Live

This is the place where we have always lived. The foothills, the plains, the rivers, the lakes, are the places where our ceremonies and sacred bundles were given to us. The plants and the animals provided our people with food and with the raw materials for clothing, shelter and tools.

This is our home and our land.
This is *Niitawahsin-nanni*

Harvesting the plants and animals meant that the Blackfoot traveled continuously throughout their territory. Although the prairies appear flat, they include many rolling hills. Tipis and other luggage were loaded on travois, which were pulled by dogs and, later, horses. These loads were unstable and would easily tip. Therefore, the Blackfoot trails wove among the undulations and coulees, leading to river crossings.

Although Blackfoot territory includes a number of large rivers, water navigation was not an important means of transportation. When large rivers needed to be crossed, people sometimes constructed circular "bull boats" from bull buffalo robes lashed to willow frames. At other times impromptu rafts were made. Many rivers had shallow ridges running across them. Ancient Blackfoot trails linked these ridges in a complex pattern across the landscape.

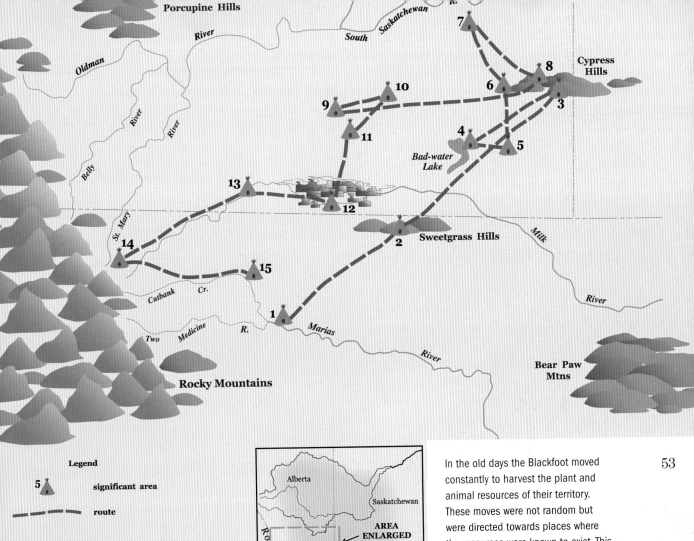

Porcupine Hills

Oldman River

South Saskatchewan

Cypress Hills

Belly River

Bad-water Lake

Sweetgrass Hills

Milk River

St. Mary

Cutbank Cr.

Marias River

Rocky Mountains

Two Medicine R.

Bear Paw Mtns

In the old days the Blackfoot moved constantly to harvest the plant and animal resources of their territory. These moves were not random but were directed towards places where the resources were known to exist. This map shows one year's travels of a clan of *Amsskaapipiikuni* in the last decade of the nineteenth century. 1. Marias River; 2. Sweet Grass Hills; 3. Cypress Hills; 4. Pakoki Lake; 5. Manyberries; 6. Buffalo Head; 7. Seven Persons; 8. Cypress Hills; 9. Long Lake; 10. Where-The-Women-Left-Their-Lodgepole: 11. Green Lake; 12. Writing-On-Stone; 13. Milk River; 14. Cutbank Creek in the foothills; 15. Cutbank Creek. In 1900 an *Amsskaapipiikuni* described one year's travel of his clan as they sought buffalo, harvested berries, and collected tipi poles.

Legend

5 🛖   significant area

– – –   route

| 0 | 50 | 100 | kilometres |
| 0 | 20 | 40 | 60 | miles |

Alberta

Saskatchewan

AREA ENLARGED

Rocky Mountains

Montana

Moving Camp

In the past, our people moved their camps as needed, to be close to wood or water, to take advantage of ripening berries and roots, and to follow the migrating herds of buffalo and other animals. During the year the attitude of our people also changed as their concerns with food meshed with the annual cycle of ceremonies.

54

Motoyi (Spring)

A time of beginnings and new life. The new year of ceremonies began as our people opened Thunder Medicine Pipe Bundles and Beaver Bundles. Our people began to look forward to *ako-katssinn* and plan for the *ookaan*.

Niipo (Summer)

Our people attended the ookaan and saw all of their relatives at the *ako-katssinn*. We moved across the open plains, harvesting the ripening berries and plentiful game.

Mokoyi (Autumn)

Work intensified as our people prepared for winter. Hunters brought more game. Our people drove buffalo into *pis-skaan* (buffalo jumps) and made plenty of "dry meat" and *moki-maani*. Beaver bundles were opened again and our people asked for help during the coming winter.

Sstoyii (Winter)

Our people moved to coulees, river bottoms and the foothills to be near plenty of wood and to be sheltered from winter storms. They were less active outside. The long nights were a time for storytelling and teaching values to the children. This was the time for all-night ceremonies.

In the old days our people could not drive to a local supermarket or hardware store to buy food and tools. Our people understood how to survive with the resources at hand. This required in-depth knowledge of ecology: Where do important plants grow? When is the best time to harvest them? Where are the best tipi poles? Where is the best place to hunt various animals? What are the best traveling routes?

The environment was the classroom; it taught our people how to live. Through the stories that the adults told of the places they had traveled, children learned where to camp, hunt and find plants.

Dogs and, later, horses helped our people as they traveled.

Imitaa: Dogs

We respect and care for *imitaa*. They have always been with us. Dogs understood the old people when they talked to them. Dogs guarded the camps and helped us hunt.

Before our people had horses, dogs carried everything. We lashed two lodgepole pine poles together, crossing them above the dog's shoulders. A platform of willow was made between the poles, behind the animal's tail. Tipi covers and other heavy gear were lashed onto this circular platform. We call these platforms *manistsii-staan*. A dog could carry a heavier load this way than with a pack.

Ponokaomitai-ksi: Horses

We have an ancient story about how horses came out of a lake and began to live among us. They were smaller than modern horses and we did not ride them or use them as pack animals.

When the horses came back to us, our people called them *Ponokaomitai-ksi* (Elk Dogs). They were as big as elk and worked for our people in the same way as dogs.

Our people first saw these big horses when the *Shoshone*, our southern neighbors, rode them into battle against the *Apatohsipiikuni* in the early 1700s. At that time our people suffered a great defeat. Soon after, they began to trade and raid for horses with their southern and western neighbors. Before long our people had large horse herds and had become great equestrians.

When horses appeared among the Blackfoot in the early 1700s, they were immediately incorporated into the culture. People became expert equestrians, trainers and breeders. The Blackfoot connected on a spiritual level with their powerful buffalo chasers and warhorses, and often kept these animals tied close to their tipis.

55

"Horses — when we break horses we take them into deep water and then ride them. When we were kids we used to collect round rocks to play with, each one represented a horse. We even had spotted rocks for pintos! They used to train horse to walk fancy, not just for fun, but because they were not easy targets that way."

ALLAN PARD,
APATOHSIPIIKUNI

Horses were superb beasts of burden. When the Blackfoot adapted their dog travois to this larger animal, they could transport heavier loads over longer distances. This enabled people to increase the size of their tipis and accumulate more material goods. As some families acquired more horses than other families, different social classes began to emerge.

Horses changed the lives of our people. They made it easier to move camp. Our people could carry larger tipis and more things. A man with a large herd of horses had prestige.

We have a special relationship with horses. We recognize their unique nature and power. Our people have medicines to keep our horses healthy and strong.

We honor our horses with elaborately decorated tack. When moving camp, people dressed in their finest clothes and outfitted their horses in bright displays. Today we carry on this tradition in parades for rodeos and Indian Days.

Iiniiksi: Buffalo

They are called buffalo, or bison, and were the most important animals to our people. The large herds covered the land.

In the summer the animals congregated in large herds on the open plains. In the winter they broke into smaller groups and sought shelter in the coulees and river bottoms. Their movements left deep tracks across the grassland. Our people followed these tracks as they moved their camps.

Thick hair on the shoulders protects the animals from freezing blizzard winds. Bison walk face-forward into storms and thus emerge from them sooner. This example teaches us to meet our challenges head-on.

The sharp horns and hoofs discourage attacks by wolves. Buffalo's legs are powerful, and they are swift and agile runners. Few of our horses could match them. Often our horses were gored when our people chased the buffalo.

The behavior of bison was never recorded in detail by the European explorers. It seems, however, that the animals came together in vast herds during the summer. In the fall and winter they split into smaller groups and drifted north into the parkland, west into the foothills, or into the larger river valleys. *The Stampede* (1883) by Frederick Verner (top); *The Stampede* (1862) by Jackob Hays (bottom).

Pis-skaan: Buffalo Jump

In the old days, before the horse returned, *pis-skaan* was very important to us. During the late summer, the winter and the spring we would lure *iiniiksi* towards steep cliffs. At these *pis-skaan*, or buffalo jumps, we could kill hundreds of animals at one time.

Sometimes, buffalo were killed singly by lone hunters. At other times hundreds of animals were run over a cliff face such as this one at Head-Smashed-In Buffalo Jump. These *pis-skaan* required the coordinated efforts of many people. Once the animals were killed, it became important to skin them and process the meat quickly, before it spoiled.

Using a *pis-skaan* was complicated, difficult and dangerous. People from many clans worked together. Early in the morning, as the sun came up, we sent our young men to bring the buffalo from their grazing grounds. Sometimes several small herds were driven together. As the animals began to move towards the cliff, they were

funneled between converging lines of low stone mounds. We stuck branches with bits of hide in the tops of these mounds. Bison have poor eyesight and these sentinels kept the animals running towards the edge.

While our young men worked among the animals, our ceremonial leaders called on the spirit of *iiniiksi* to pity us and make our *pis-skaan* successful. Men who had the rights to the buffalo-design tipis, *iinisskimm* (buffalo calling stones) and Beaver Bundles gathered together to pray for success and sing their buffalo songs. The *pis-skaan* succeeded only if the ceremony was properly conducted.

The Importance of *Iiniiski*

Iiniiski gave our people almost everything they needed. We used the buffalo's strong hide to make tipi covers, containers, shields, and soles for our moccasins. Heavy fur robes served as blankets and overcoats during the coldest weather. Sinew from the backbone was strong thread. The bladders made good containers for water and soup. Hoofs were our tipi "doorbells" and rattles. Our people boiled hoofs for glue and for fixatives for paint on our tipis, shields and containers.

60

Buffalo, or plains bison, covered the Plains in countless numbers and were the most important animal in the Blackfoot world. Food, clothing, shelter and tools all came from the buffalo.

Bison meat was very important to our people's diet. Much of the meat was cut into thin strips and hung to dry in the sun. This natural processing was much healthier than our modern use of chemicals. The raw kidneys were a real treat. For a balanced diet our people made blood soup and blood sausage, which provided iron and other base elements.

Today, many of our ceremonies to honor the *iiniiksi* continue to help us. Our ceremonies with *iinisskimm* (buffalo calling stones) and buffalo-design tipis are still passed on. Dried buffalo tongues given out by the Holy Woman at the *ookaan* bring us good health throughout the year.

Our split horn headdress with the eagle feather trailer honors *iiniiksi*. The horns and *aapaiai* (white weasel) make up the head. The eagle feathers are the spine. A man who owns a headdress such as this can call on the strength and power of the buffalo.

We owed our entire way of life to *iiniiksi*.

Plants

Our world is filled with plants. Our ancestors knew all the plants that grew here and had uses for almost every one of them. Some were used for tools, some for food, others for medicine. Often we moved camp to be near a spot where an important plant had ripened and was ready to be collected.

Our tipi poles, tripods, backrests, bowls, bows and arrows were all made from different kinds of wood. Lodgepole pine makes the best tipi poles; it grows in the foothills of the Rockies, the Cypress Hills and the Porcupine Hills. Bow wood (chokecherry) was collected only when the sap was running. Saskatoon branches were our arrow shafts. Bowls were made from burls growing on cottonwood trees.

Plants were a key part of our diet. Berries and roots supplied us with the vitamins and minerals that kept us healthy. Some plants provided important enzymes to help our people digest meat and make optimal use of fats and proteins. Berries were especially important, providing many vitamins and nutrients. Different berries ripen at different times, and we often moved camp to be near a berry as it was ready for harvesting.

We also make medicine from plants. Some of these medicines are common knowledge. Others are gifts from the Spirit Beings, and we need special rights transferred to us before we can use them.

We do not use as many native plants today. Our environment has changed greatly; many plants are now more rare or have completely disappeared. Our knowledge of medicines may be disappearing as the old people depart without teaching the young people. Our health is suffering as a result.

62

There are special places in Blackfoot territory where the ancient stories of our culture happened. This is where the Spirit Beings changed into human form and gave us our sacred ceremonies. These places provide physical evidence that the events really happened and are part of Blackfoot history. Sacred places connect the Blackfoot to our territory, are part of our identity and are the basis of our claim to this territory.

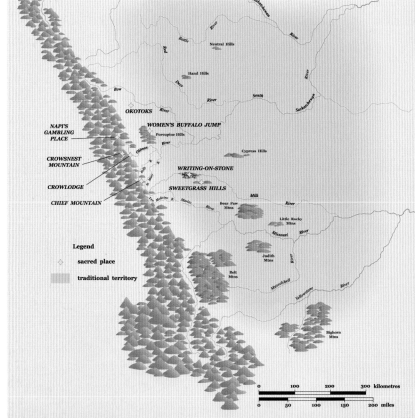

Ninastako, also called Chief Mountain, is the home of Thunder. When he stole the wife of a Blackfoot man, he took her to his home inside this mountain. Raven came from his home at Crowsnest Mountain and fought with Thunder on the slopes of *Ninastako*. *Ninastako* means "the mountain that stands apart" reflecting the separateness of this mountain from the surrounding range.

Our Sacred Places

Our sacred sites are places where significant things happened to our ancestors. This is where the ancient stories took place. These sites are uniquely important to us. They tell us that our ancient stories are true. They tell us that we belong to this place in a way that no other human being can.

Our sacred geography shows us our path through life. By following this path, our people will live long and productive lives.

The badlands of the Milk River Valley in southern Alberta contain the ancient picture writing of the Blackfoot. Some of these images recount historical events, while others refer to ancient stories and to sacred gifts from the Spirit Beings. This place tells us much about the essence of the Blackfoot culture, but few individuals understand the images on these rocks.

Chapter 5

Our Relationships with Other People

(Previous Page) *Siksika* parading through Calgary, 1912; trade goods used by the Blackfoot (inset).

Other *Nii-tsi-ta-pii-ksi*

Our territory had almost everything our people needed. However, there were some resources that were not present. Our people were part of a continent-wide trading network that existed thousands of years before the Europeans arrived. The stone here is not very good for making tools, so we obtained better materials from our neighbors across the Rocky Mountains, south to the Teton Mountains, and east to the middle Missouri River area. Our ancestors also traded shell ornaments. Dentalium (a small shellfish from the Pacific coast) and cowrie shells (from the Gulf of Mexico) were traded throughout the continent.

Our people were not interested in dominating others or forcing our way of life on them. They coexisted with their neighbors just as they coexisted with the rest of Creation.

Peace treaties were made before trading took place. These treaties ensured that the exchange was done in the spirit of goodwill. It was our custom to exchange gifts as a sign of friendship. Everyone also smoked a pipe and asked *Ihtsi-pai-tapi-yopa* to witness the treaty and help everyone live up to their obligations.

Although our people traded with their neighbors they did not tolerate others living or hunting in their homeland. Our men were known as fierce warriors who were fearless in battle as they kept other people out of *Niitawahsin-nanni*.

Napikowann: The Fur Trade: 1740–1830

When the first fur traders came to our territory, their behavior seemed strange and inappropriate. We did not understand them; they reminded our people of the *Napi* (Old Man) stories. We called them *Napikowann*.

The *Napikowann* came from the north, east and south. They competed with one another for business. They wanted buffalo meat, *moki-maani* and furs. In return they gave our people tobacco, guns, steel knives and arrowheads, blankets, cloth and many ornaments. They also gave our people liquor.

The Trading Ceremony

Our traditional protocol has always been important to us. When our people met to trade with *Napikowann*, they always made a treaty first. A pipe was smoked in friendship and *Ihtsi-pai-tapi-yopa* was called on to help us work well together. Then our people gave the *Napikowann* leader some of our best furs. In return, their leader gave gifts to our leaders. Often, alcohol too was given.

We had no tradition of making or using alcohol, so our people easily became drunk. They often fought and killed one another while intoxicated. The alcohol was a mixture of rum, gunpowder and other toxic ingredients that slowly killed or blinded those who drank it. But the alcohol was addictive and many of our people were caught in its snare.

Fort Edmonton was the largest fur trade post built near the Blackfoot territory. Situated on a promontory on the north bank of the North Saskatchewan River, this post commanded an excellent view of the river valley and the river crossing places. Moreover, the river linked the fort with the rest of the Hudson's Bay Company's trading network to the north and east. From an 1872 engraving by Edward Whymper, *View of Fort Edmonton*.

"The white people thought they were coming into empty land. We had a life and a system going here and it's still ongoing."

PAT PROVOST,
APATOHSIPIIKUNI

Leaders

Some of our men were more willing to trade than others. They visited the traders often, sometimes bringing many people with them. The traders believed that these men were leaders of all our people and gave them many gifts.

Napikowann did not understand our system of leadership. They expected us to have a single leader who acted on everyone's behalf. The *Napikowann* could not grasp our flexible leadership style and the need for consensus in decision-making.

Over time, the *Napikowann*'s approach to our leaders greatly affected our society. Men who regularly traded at the posts became wealthy in new goods and controlled access to the traders. Some began making arrangements with foreign governments. Our people's traditional authority was undermined and the authority of a single spokesman was enhanced.

The northwestern Plains was the last part of North America in which fur trading posts were established. The Blackfoot welcomed the presence of traders but ensured that no long-term trading posts were built in their territory. Consequently, these posts were situated along the periphery of the territory. Traders were also inhibited from crossing the mountains westward to trade with the *Ktunaxa* and other Native groups. Thus, firearms were kept away from the Blackfoot's traditional enemies, resulting in a strategic advantage in battle and trade.

Furs

Our people had always coexisted with the Spirit Beings who had shown them how to live and had given our people food and shelter. With their help, we quickly adapted our hunting strategies to the new demand for furs and hides.

Our people did not depend on the new goods obtained through trade. Rather, we incorporated and

Whitemud Brooke House
Fort Edmonton, Fort Augustus
Buckingham House, Fort George
Nelson House
Fort Vermilion
North Saskatchewan
Boggy Hall
Manchester House
Carlton House
Turtle Fort
Fort Carlton
Upper Hudson's House
Rocky Mtn House, Acton House
Battle River
River
South Branch Houses
Neutral Hills
Pigeon's House
Red Deer River
Hand Hills
Bow River
Chesterfield House
South Saskatchewan River
Porcupine Hills
Oldman
Cypress Hills
Belly
St. Mary
CANADA
U.S.A.
The Medicine R.
Marias River
Milk River
Bear Paw Mtns
Fort McKenzie
Little Rocky Mtns
River
Fort Union
Missouri River
Legend
fur trade post
Judith Mtns
Musselshell River
traditional territory
Belt Mtns
Yellowstone River
Bighorn Mtns

0   100   200   300 kilometres
0   50   100   150   200 miles

adapted those we found useful. Steel knives and metal arrowheads lasted longer than those made of stone. The copper and iron pots made cooking easier. Blankets and cloth were brighter and easier to sew than hides. Beads and other ornaments were a novelty.

Firearms

Firearms were one of the most important things *Napikowann* brought to our people. Muskets made hunting easier, although the early ones were fragile and the firing mechanisms often broke. Eventually, the firearms were made sturdier and became more important in our hunting. Our people shortened the barrel so they could hunt from horseback.

Guns also changed the way our people fought. Before *Napikowann* came, our people faced their enemies using large, heavy shields for protection. They could shoot arrows at one another all day with few casualties. Firearms made the conflicts riskier. More young men died in battle.

After our enemies the *Shoshone* rode horses into battle and defeated us, we were eager for revenge. We visited some Cree, who were then our allies, and asked for their help. They readily joined us, and brought muskets they had obtained from the English traders. When we met the *Shoshone*, we had a great victory.

The Blackfoot modified many trade goods to make them more usable in a mobile, equestrian culture. Blankets were sewn into hooded coats called *capotes*. Musket barrels were sawed off for easier manipulation while on horseback. The barrels were also flattened into hide scrapers with serrated blades. Pieces of copper were flattened and rolled into small cones; when these cones were hung on shirt and dress fringes, they tinkled with a musical tone.

Disease

Napikowann also brought disease:

- smallpox (*Sika-piksinn*)
- measles (*Aapikssinn*)
- whooping cough
- tuberculosis (*Isttsikssaa-isskinaan*)
- influenza

The newcomers brought more than trade goods; they also carried disease. Blackfoot Winter Counts record the important events of each year with pictographs. The Count kept by Bull Plume, an *Apatohsipiikuni*, began several generations before he was born. It records devastating epidemics of smallpox, measles, tuberculosis and other diseases. These ravaged almost every generation.

Every fifteen to twenty years — each generation, in other words — a new epidemic spread through our people's camps. Each time, a half to three-quarters of our people died: infants, children, adults, our old people. Families were devastated. The knowledge of our ceremonial leaders and old people began to disappear.

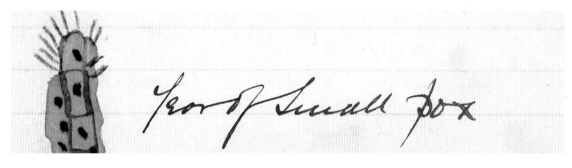

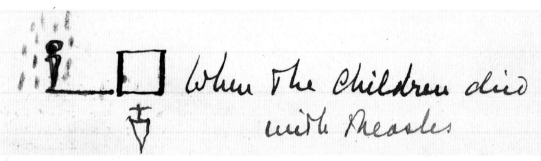

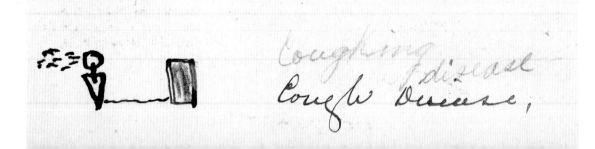

Our people had traditional ways of curing diseases, with herbs and prayers, but these were powerless against the new diseases. Our people had no way to fight these new, invisible enemies.

Whisky Trade: 1830–1880

As more *Napikowann* came into our territory, changes happened that Our people could not control or resist. These newcomers did not want furs, dry meat, or *moki-maani*; all they wanted was tanned buffalo hides. These were sent to Fort Benton, Montana, where they were loaded onto steamboats and shipped up the Missouri River to St. Louis and the eastern United States. The thick hides were made into robes for sleighs and winter coats.

Whisky was the most important commodity these Americans traded. The effects were disastrous. Brothers killed brothers in drunken brawls. Men began to beat their wives. Some men sold their wives to traders in exchange for whisky and food.

And the buffalo herds became smaller.

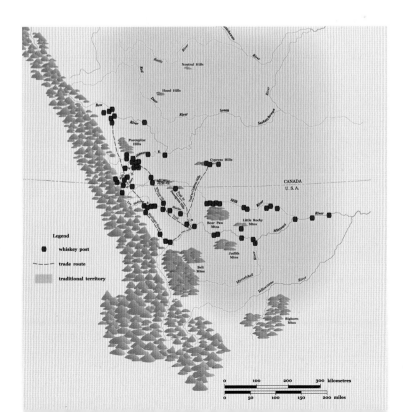

By the 1830s the European and American demand for buffalo robes surpassed that for beaver and other fur. It was impractical to ship these heavy robes by canoe and boat to Montreal or Hudson Bay. It was more efficient to transport them by cart to Fort Benton, Montana, where they were loaded onto riverboats. The routes from Fort Benton followed the old Blackfoot trails.

For buffalo robes, the Americans traded primarily whisky. This rotgut mixture of alcohol, pepper, gunpowder and other toxins poisoned the Blackfoot. Bull Plume's Winter Count symbol recounts the death toll from the whisky trade.

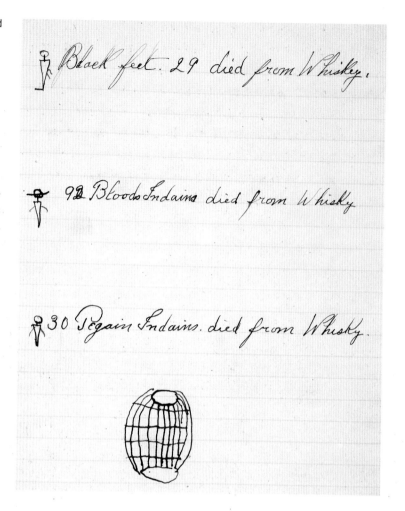

Black feet. 29 died from Whisky.

92 Bloods Indains died from Whisky

30 Pegain Indains. died from Whisky.

Ii-moh-ksi-so-ka-sii-ksi (Redcoats): The North West Mounted Police

Our people found the first Redcoats wandering near *Katoyissiksi* (Sweet Grass Hills). They were lost and starving. Our people took pity on them. Bull Head, one of the Apatohsipiikuni leaders, said they could camp in the Oldman River bottom for the winter.

They never left.

At first our people thought the Redcoats were helping us. They chased the whisky traders back to the United States. Canada, at least, became a sanctuary from liquor.

But soon the Redcoats began enforcing their own laws. Hunting was restricted. Our people could no longer defend their territory against other First Nations.

Other Native people — Cree, Dakota, Lakota, Nakoda, Crow, Nez Perce and Metis — moved into our territory as the buffalo became scarce across the Plains. There were not enough buffalo to share. Our people began to fight with their neighbors more often. Guns were better now, and battles became even more deadly.

The North West Mounted Police were sent to western Canada in 1873 after violence erupted at the whisky trading posts in the Cypress Hills. They were empowered to evict unlicensed American traders and restore sobriety to the Canadian prairies. This painting is by R.B. Nevitt, a surgeon with the NWMP In their early days.

Treaties with Governments

The governments of Canada and the United States each
signed treaties with our people. They wanted our land. We
understood the treaties differently.

Mek-yāpy
Red Dye
Piïgan warrior

O-nes-Tah-stäm-mek
white Bull
Pagan Chief

Lame Bull Treaty (1855)

The 1849 gold strike in California changed the face of western North America. In 1840, one thousand Americans crossed the Plains from St. Louis, Missouri, to California.

Ne-tannāy. The only chief
or
STām-yekh-sás-ci-cay. Lame Bull
Piegan Chief

American migration across the Plains increased phenomenally during the 1840s, and in 1853 an exploratory survey party examined possible railroad routes along the Missouri River drainage. This was Blackfoot territory, and many battles were erupting as other Native people encroached on these rich buffalo grounds. In 1855, Isaac Stevens presided over a treaty among all Native groups that met on the buffalo plains. These drawings are the only images of the Blackfoot people who attended those negotiations. From right: Red Dye; White Bull: Lame Bull.

By 1877 the bison had almost disappeared and diseases had depopulated the Blackfoot. The Canadian government wanted to open the land for settlement. Treaty 7 was negotiated between the government and the *Siksika*, *Kainai* and *Apatohsipiikuni*, as well as the *Tsuu T'ina* and *Nakoda*. R.B. Nevitt's portrayal of the NWMP camp reflects the strong police presence. Many Blackfoot people believe this was meant to intimidate their leaders.

In 1849, ten thousand Americans crossed this same path. Game was diminished and Native People were crushed together. Conflicts and violence escalated.

The United States government wanted to ensure safe passage for the migrants, so they commissioned Isaac Stephens to negotiate a peace treaty with all of the Plains First Nations. We call this the Lame Bull Treaty, after one of our leaders who was present at the negotiations.

Our people agreed to peaceful coexistence with their neighbors. In return, the United States government agreed to recognize the vast extent of our territory and to keep settlers and other First Nations away from our land.

Before long, however, the U.S. government began reducing the size of our territory. As more ranchers and miners arrived, Executive Orders from the president ceded our land to the federal government.

A few of our people tried to fight back. The so-called Blackfoot War lasted from 1865 to 1870. It ended when U.S. Cavalry Colonel E.M. Baker attacked a camp of *Amsskaapipiikuni* whom he believed were hostile. In fact, they were a peaceable camp consisting mostly of women, children and old people recovering from smallpox.

Treaty 7 (1877)

In 1670, King Charles II of England granted the Hudson's Bay Company. exclusive rights to the land and resources of all the territory that drains into Hudson Bay. No one consulted or informed our people who were living there.

In 1870, the Hudson's Bay Company sold these lands and resources to

"The treaties changed us. History starts with everything we have today. It starts with the treaty and the rights given to us. The treaties still exist with us, but it is written down incorrectly and it is therefore hard to understand."

LOUISE CROP EARED WOLF,
KAINAI

the new Dominion of Canada. Again, no one consulted or informed our people who were living there.

The Canadian government quickly set about signing treaties with the First Nations living in the southern part of the newly acquired territory. The government wished to secure legal title to the land and end any claims the First Nations might have. This would pave the way for the settlement of the West by waves of European immigrants.

The Canadian government wrote in Treaty 7:

> And whereas the said Commissioners have proceeded to negotiate a Treaty with said Indians; and the same has been finally agreed upon and concluded as follows, that is to say: the Blackfoot, Blood, Piegan, Sarcee, Stony, and other Indians inhabiting the District hereinafter more fully described and defined, do hereby cede, release, surrender, and yield up to the Government of Canada for Her Majesty the Queen and her successors for ever, all their rights, titles, and privileges whatsoever to the lands ...

"Cede, release, surrender, yield, rights, title, privileges" — what did these words mean to our people? How could the Canadians translate British legal concepts into a culture that had no concept of land ownership? Our people had always coexisted with all of Creation. We had no "title" to the land, and our people's "rights" to coexist had been granted by the *Ihtsi-pai-tapi-yopa*. Our people could not comprehend these terms.

Our oral tradition tells us that the leaders did not sign a land transfer agreement with the Canadian government. They agreed to live peacefully with the new immigrants and asked for their help in adjusting to a new way of living. We cannot make a treaty unless all parties share a pipe with *Ihtsi-pai-tapi-yopa* as witness; and our leaders did not share a pipe with the government representative.

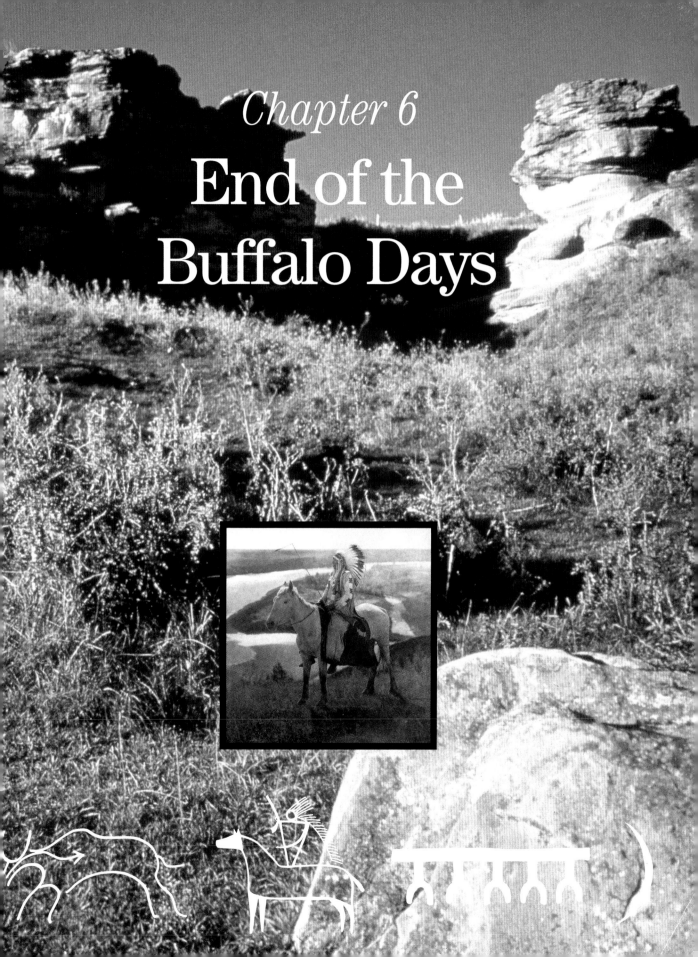

Chapter 6
End of the Buffalo Days

We thought we would have more time: more time to learn about the newcomers who were filling our land; more time to learn about farming and ranching; more time to adjust to these new ways. But by 1879 the buffalo had disappeared. The governments of Canada and the United States told our people they must live on reserves if they wanted help. Our people had to obey laws that made no sense to their way of thinking. But our people were starving and could not resist these changes.

We gave up the old ways and moved to the reserves and reservations.

Kinnonna: Indian Agents

When our people moved to the reserves, a new, all-powerful authority emerged: the Indian agent (*kinnonna*). These men were appointed by the Canadian government

The people soon found their lives ruled by the Indian agent. These Canadian government officials were charged with ensuring that the Blackfoot left their past traditions behind and adopted the white customs. These men monitored all aspects of Blackfoot life.

and given complete authority over the lives of our people. Indian agents could limit or refuse to give out rations.

In Canada, Indian agents issued passes that permitted people to leave the reserve for three days; any person caught off the reserve without a valid pass was sent to jail for thirty days. Indian agents issued permits to sell crops and livestock. They made sure the children went to school. Indian agents ran our council meetings and often selected the chiefs and members of council.

Indian agents implemented government policy, regardless of whether or not it benefitted our people.

Houses

The old reserve houses were not like our tipis. They were square, and air did not circulate well within them. There was no insulation, so the houses were very cold in the

"The devil can corner you in a house, but not in a tipi."

HERMAN YELLOW
OLD WOMAN,
SIKSIKA

Life for the Blackfoot was very different by the late 1880s. The people were moved onto reserves and reservations, where they were told to live in houses rather than tipis. The first houses were built of logs and ventilation was poor. Many of these dwellings became breeding grounds for disease.

81

winter. Many of our people became sick from epidemics of whooping cough and tuberculosis.

At first, people settled near their clan relatives and built houses facing east. They tried to camp as they had always done. As our people began to rely on rations, they moved closer to the Indian agent's office and the ration house. Some people began to lose touch with their clan relations.

Rations

"In 1890 nearly one-quarter of Amsskaapipiikuni starved to death on Ghost Ridge."

— David Hurst Thomas,
Archaeologist

The bison had disappeared by 1880, and drought and a worldwide economic depression curtailed a successful transition to agriculture. People were forced to rely on government rations for survival. This increased their dependency and enhanced the control of the Indian agent. It was yet one more demoralizing blow.

When the buffalo, the mainstay of our existence, disappeared, our people tried farming and ranching. The government regulations made this hard. The drought and hard winters of the 1890s wiped out the crops and herds.

Our people began to rely on government aid for survival. But the governments complained about the high cost of feeding our people and cut back on the food supply.

Sometimes the food was rotten. The beef and pork were often spoiled and the flour full of weevils. Once, on the Blood Reserve, when the meat was salted with lime, many people became sick and died.

The ration food was not good for our people. They had always eaten sun-cured meat and wild plants. Now, the commercial food made them sick. To this day, we have health problems caused by the change in our diet.

In 1901 the *Siksika* were brought to an area near Calgary, Alberta, to greet the Duke and Duchess of Cornwall (later King George V and Queen Mary). Medals were to be presented to the chiefs, and the *Siksika* were to "show off" their traditional dress and dance. However, adequate rations had not been issued for several months. A number of men readied themselves and their horses for war. They planned to attack the royal couple if food was not forthcoming. The government managed to find food before trouble erupted.

Farming on the Prairies during the nineteenth century was difficult enough with ploughs and horses, but it became nearly impossible for the Blackfoot when the Canadian government invoked the Peasant Farm Policy. Men were reduced to sowing seed by hand and harvesting their pitiful crops with hand tools. The rationale was that this gave Native people a better understanding of the land.

Farming and Ranching

Our people persevered and were successful in farming and ranching. The Wolf Trail had taught them how to work together and share resources, and these principles were easily adapted to farming and ranching. They used their knowledge of horses to develop fine teams. Some of our people became very successful.

Our homesteader neighbors felt threatened by our success. Some were jealous; others wanted our land. So, in 1889, the Canadian government established the Peasant Farm Policy. It was decided that each adult could farm only one acre and care for one or two cows. Our people were allowed to use only simple tools, such as hoes, rakes, cradles, sickles and flails. They were not allowed to work together cooperatively. The land that was not used was rented, sold, or given to neighboring ranchers and farmers. This policy lasted until 1896. It was a complete failure.

By the 1920s the effects of government industrial schools were being felt. A few individuals became successful ranchers, using community pastures for their herds. Farming was still difficult and much of the land was either leased to non-Native neighbors or kept as hayfields. Few Blackfoot could afford the expensive steam tractors used to drive the threshing machines. This scene shows *Kainai* using steam tractors that they purchased with their own funds.

Our people's agricultural efforts were also hampered by the oppressive control of the Indian agent. He had absolute control over all aspects of our lives. Our people could not buy seeds, sell crops or ship livestock without his permission. Sometimes he bought seed that had not been properly cleaned, so some years we sowed more weeds than wheat. If the agent's judgment was poor, our people lost money on the sales.

Residential Schools

Schools were supposed to teach our people how to read and write, and give them the skills to live among the newcomers. Instead, schools destroyed our family structure, our sense of belonging and our identity.

Schools almost destroyed us.

During the late nineteenth century the United States government sent our children across the country to the

Carlyle School in Pennsylvania. Later, residential schools were built on the Blackfeet Reservation in Montana.

The Canadian government's solution was to establish residential schools on the reserves. Religious organizations were contracted to establish these schools, with the Anglicans and Roman Catholics predominating among the *Siksika*, *Kainai* and *Apatohsipiikuni*.

Government and religious leaders recognized that the only way to break down our culture and assimilate our people was to remove the children from their homes, so children were put into residential schools for ten or eleven months each year. Our traditional practices and language were repressed, and students caught using either were punished. Boys and girls were physically separated and

After ten years, enrollment had increased at the residential schools such as this one at North Camp, *Siksika*. Uniforms reflected non-Native styles of dress, and stern looks and physical punishment from the teachers drove Blackfoot traditions into hiding. These children began to lose their connection with their families. Too often, there was nothing to fill the resulting void.

The residential schools were chronically underfunded. Children like these *Piikuni* grew much of their own food and even stuffed their own mattresses with straw. The instructors believed that this taught the children self-sufficiency. Many former students see this as added repression in an already terrible situation.

did not learn how to interact with and respect one another. Children were taken from their families, depriving them of the opportunity to learn parenting skills, love, and respect.

Sexual and physical abuse by staff and students was widespread. The children were helpless. They learned institutional behavior — how to bully the young and weak. They learned to treat each other with contempt and violence.

Our people began to forget the lessons of the Wolf Trail. They began to forget how to coexist with all of Creation.

Residential schools created many dysfunctional people with low self-esteem, and these people in turn created a dysfunctional society. This process has now been going on for five or six generations.

The healing will take a long time.

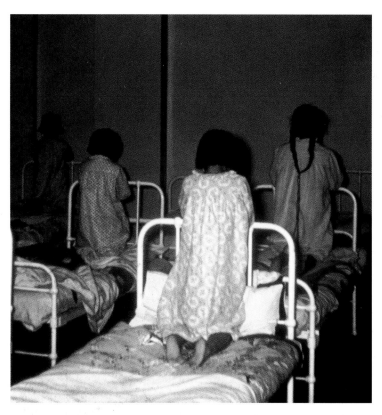

Residential schools, such as Old Sun at *Siksika*, were religious-based and modeled after European boarding schools. Few things were more foreign to the Blackfoot way of child rearing than the large, stark dormitories. These were lonely places for the children, who found neither welcome nor comfort.

At St. Paul's Residential School on the Blood Reserve, staff lived in surroundings that were familiar and comfortable. This not only differentiated staff from students, it also separated the white officials from their Blackfoot neighbors. The economic differences underscored the impoverishment of the Blackfoot and excluded them from control over their own fate.

Our Disappearing Land

The treaties defined the territory that the Canadian and United States governments agreed would be ours. But these lands have been steadily taken from us. Some areas passed into other hands as the reserve boundaries were being surveyed. Other parcels seem to have been given away. Sometimes we were forced to sell land to pay for government programs.

United States

Our 1855 treaty with the United States government acknowledged our hunting rights to vast areas in what is now Montana. However, several decrees by the president took away most of this land.

In 1887, the Dawes Allotment Act became law. Each adult tribal member became eligible to receive full legal title for a 320-acre plot of land. When the allotment was granted, the individual gave up their rights as a Native American. In 1919, the Homestead Act gave individuals an additional eighty acres of land. These plots of land were to be our farms, and our means of assimilation into mainstream society.

Our people soon discovered that they were subject to property

The land guaranteed for Blackfoot use in the 1855 treaty was quickly reduced in size. Land was appropriated or sold for development as ranches or goldfields. In Canada the size of the reserves was based on population. Some of this land was later sold, some was appropriated, and some of the promised land was excluded as the reserve boundaries were surveyed.

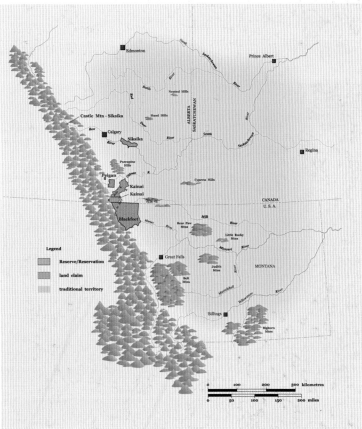

Legend
Reserve/Reservation
land claim
traditional territory

90

taxes. When the farms were not successful, the land was confiscated by the local county to pay the tax arrears. Much of our reservation was bought by non-Natives. This has created a checkerboard of land ownership, making it difficult for us to manage our resources. It has also created deeply felt tensions.

Canada

Kainai have an oral tradition that says Red Crow stipulated their reserve would stretch from the Oldman River to the U.S.–Canada border and from St. Mary's River to the Rocky Mountains. This reserve now ends at Cardston and is bounded by the Waterton and Belly rivers. We do not know how or when this new boundary was established.

In 1901 the government began trying to convince *Siksika* to sell a vast area of land. They told our people that the money would be kept in trust and reduce poverty on the reserve. Also, the land would be a welcome home for the newly arrived immigrants from Europe. For many years *Siksika* refused. In 1908 their rations were withheld, partly to "encourage" our people to farm, partly to coerce them to sell the land. A vote was held in 1910 and the Indian agent declared that the people had agreed to the sale of 125,000 acres. Many of us still question the accuracy of the vote, and the sale caused bad feelings that have lasted for decades.

Treaty 7 allocated timber reserves for the *Siksika*, *Kainai* and *Apatohsipiikuni*, where they could harvest logs to build homes and for firewood. Early in the twentieth century a woman died at the *Siksika* timber limit and the area was avoided for many years. When the *Siksika* tried to return, they found that the timber reserve had become part of Banff National Park.

The *Apatohsipiikuni* reserve too has become smaller over the years. Our oral traditions tell of large parcels of land that were let out for grazing but were never given back or paid for.

Images of Us

In 1910 the United States government passed legislation creating Glacier National Park in northwestern Montana. They wanted to purchase all of our lands near the mountains to create this park. Our leaders negotiated as best they could but settled for less money than they wanted.

The Great Northern Railroad supported the creation of the park. In 1911 the railroad opened a series of resort lodges. These quickly became attractions for wealthy tourists from around the world. Our people were paid to camp at the lodges and dress in our traditional buckskin

When Guy Weadick promoted the first Calgary Exhibition and Stampede in 1912, the Blackfoot figured prominently. *Siksika* and other Native groups were brought to Calgary and set up in a camp near the rodeo grounds. This brought an element of the Wild West show and made the Stampede unique among rodeos.

(Previous Page) The *Siksika*, *Apatohsipiikuni* and *Kainai*, along with the *Nakoda* and *Tsuu T'ina*, were eventually moved to a special area of the exhibition grounds, which came to be known as the "tipi village." Here, dignitaries and other visitors often had their first encounter with Native people. Daily parades on horseback were an opportunity for Native people to present themselves in their best traditional attire.

clothes. The authorities who had tried to eradicate our culture were now using us to promote their tourist destinations.

Our people were also prominent in the first Calgary Stampede, in 1912. Guy Weadick, the promoter, arranged for *Siksika* to travel to Calgary, where they camped near the rodeo grounds, although federal regulations limited off-reserve visits to three days. Weadick obtained special permission for a longer stay.

We were used to create a Wild West atmosphere. This Indian Village soon became an integral part of the Stampede. Our presence remains important to this day.

An important event at the "tipi village" is the judging of the tipi interiors. The space is arranged as though it was lived in, with clothes, parfleche, dry meat and other items hung as they would have been in the past. This has become a highly competitive aspect of the "village."

Chapter 7
We Are Meant to Be
Nii-tsi-ta-pii-ksi

Our traditional values are still important to us. A century of forced assimilation has failed. Many of us still speak our language; our ceremonies continue and our beliefs are strong.

Government control over our affairs has left a legacy of institutions that do not work. Our governments are tied to federal bureaucratic regulations. The educational system has improved, but the curriculum and teaching methods do not support our cultural ways. The justice and welfare systems fail to adequately address our social problems.

Now we are developing our own systems. We are using our traditional values and protocols to create more meaningful governments, schools, and welfare and justice systems. As our people see their own traditions reflected in these institutions, they will support them. Community support is essential for success.

It is a big challenge to achieve these goals. High-tech entertainment lures our youth away from learning their own language and traditions. The lack of an economic base draws our people away from the reserves/reservations and the community that supports them.

If we are to continue as *Nii-tsi-ta-pii-ksi*, we must take control of the tools of oppression and combine them with our own values to make tools that can shape our future.

The *Nii-tsi-ta-pii-ksi* you meet today carry with them ancient traditions, a long history and modern challenges. All of us are individuals who must find our own blend of these features and fashion our own way in the world. We cannot fit into a single, stereotyped image.

If we are all to live together, we must learn to understand and accept each other as individuals.

"Children are being taught our language, culture, and history in schools. It is our own people who are teaching and educating them. They are fluent in Blackfoot and raised in our traditions, but also have MAs."

DONNA WEASEL CHILD,
SIKSIKA

96

Glossary of Blackfoot Terms

The Blackfoot language is structured very differently than English. Consequently, it is difficult to find exact translations for Blackfoot words. In addition, there are few widely accepted conventions for spelling. We have agreed upon the versions of the words that are presented here so that the non-Blackfoot speaker might gain some insight to our language and thus to our culture. We have chosen to hyphenate the syllables to help with the pronunciation.

Aapaiai	Weasel with its coat in the white phase; ermine
Aapikssinn	Measles
Ako-katssinn	Circle camp; when all camp in one place
Amsskaapipiikuni	Southern Peigan; also referred to as Peigan and Blackfeet by some Euro-American writers and artists. This part of the larger group who call themselves *Piikuni* live in northwestern Montana
Apatohsipiikuni	Northern Peigan; part of the larger group who call themselves *Piikuni* and who live in Alberta, Canada
Ihtsi-pai-tapi-yopa	Essence of All Life; Creator
Ii-moh-ksi-so-ka-sii-ksi	Redcoats
Iinisskimm	Buffalo calling stone
Iinnii	Buffalo (singular)
Imitaa	Dog
Iniiksiit	Buffalo (plural)
Ipisowahsi	Morning star
Isttsikssaa-isskinaant	Tuberculosis
Kainait	Many Leaders; also called the Bloods
Katoyissa	Blood clot
Katoyissiksit	Sweet Grass Hills (more properly, Sweet Pine Hills)

Kinnonnat	Indian agent
Kokomi-kisommt	Moon
Ksahkomi-tapiiksi	Earth beings
Ksiistsi-komm	Thunder
Ksisk-staki	Beaver
Makoi-yohsokoyi	Wolf Trail
Makoiyi	Wolf
Manistsi-staan	Travois made from tipi poles
Minipoka	Favored children
Moki-maani	Dry meat, berries and fat mixed together; pemmican
Mokoyi	Autumn
Motoyi	Spring
Naa-to-yi-ta-piiksi	Spirit Beings
Napi	Old man
Napikowann	White man
Natosi	Sun
Niitsitapiisinni	Our way of life
Nii-tsi-ta-pii-ksi	Real people
Niipo	Summer
Niitoy-yiss	Tipi
Ninastako	Chief Mountain
Niitawahsin-nanni	Our Land
Niitsi-poi-yksi	People who speak the real language
Oki	Hello
Omahkai-stow	Raven
Omahksi-spatsi-koyii	Great Sand Hills
Ookaan	Sun dance
Otahkoi-tah-tayi	Yellow River (Yellowstone or Musselshell River)

Peigan	A term that refers one of the three groups of Blackfoot-speaking people who live in southern Alberta. They are closely related to the *Amsskaapipiikuni* (Piegan; Blackfeet) in northwestern Montana. They refer to themselves as *Apatohsipiikuni*.
Piegan	A term used by Americans to refer to Blackfoot-speaking people whose traditional homeland is northwestern Montana. The name "Blackfeet" is also used in reference to this group, who are part of the larger *Piikuni* division of the *Niitsitapi*. It is also spelled Peigan, even though Peigan generally refers to those who live in Canada. They refer to themselves as *Amsskaapipiikuni*.
Pis-skaan	Buffalo jump
Ponoka	Elk
Ponoka-si-sahta	Elk River (North Saskatchewan River)
Ponoko-mitta	Horse
Sao-kitapiiksi	Plains people
Sika-piksinn	Smallpox
Siksika	Blackfoot
Sootsi-maan	Parfleche or rawhide container
Soyii-tapiiksi	Water beings
Spiitsii	High River, Alberta
Spomi-tapiiksi	Above beings
Sstoyii	Winter

Image Credits and Bibliography

Front Cover, Main Image: The Tipi Liners, Livingstone Range, southwestern Alberta, photograph by Anita Dammer © Glenbow Museum

Front Cover, Inset (left to right): Tipi Pegs, Siksika, mid 20th century, black birch, Collection of Glenbow Museum; T.J. Hileman, Weasel Tail, Blood [Kainai] [detail], 1927, Collection of Glenbow Archives, NB-21-38; Blackfoot Artifacts, late 19th to mid 20th century, Collection of Glenbow Museum; Photographer Unknown, Blackfoot [Siksika] in Full Regalia, Dancing at Cluny, Alberta [detail], August 28, 1967, Collection of Glenbow Archives, NA-2557-80

Back Cover (top to bottom): Dress [detail], Siksika, late 19th century, buckskin, glass, cloth and sinew, Collection of Glenbow Museum, AF 1257; Reiss T., Two Blackfeet [Amsskaapipiikuni] Girls [detail], ca. 1930s, Collection of Glenbow Archives, NA-5425-53; Frederick Arthur Verner, The Stampede [detail], 1883, oil on canvas, Collection of Glenbow Museum, Purchased, 1955, 55.28; Edward S. Curtis, Peigan [Amsskaapipiikuni] Painted Lodges [detail], 1900, Collection of Glenbow Archives, NA-1700-141

Inside Cover: Woman's Buffalo Jump, southwestern Alberta, photograph by Anita Dammer © Glenbow Museum

Table of Contents: Arnold Lupson, Blackfoot [Siksika] Tipis, ca. 1930s, Collection of Glenbow Archives, NA-667-202

Chapter 1, Main Image: Edward S. Curtis, Peigan [Amsskaapipiikuni] Tipi Encampment, 1905, Collection of Glenbow Archives, NA-1700-143; Inset: Writing-On-Stone Provincial Park [Áísínai'pi], photograph by Anita Dammer © Glenbow Museum

Page 11: (clockwise from top left): Edward S. Curtis, Double Runner, Peigan [Amsskaapipiikuni], 1900, Collection of Glenbow Archives, NA-1700-140; Edward S. Curtis, Stsimaki ("Reluctant-to-be-Woman"), Blood [Kainai], 1926, Collection of Glenbow Library; Edward S. Curtis, New Chest, Peigan [Amsskaappipiikuni], 1910, Collection of Glenbow Archives, NA-1700-146; Edward S. Curtis, Two Bear Woman, Peigan [Amsskaapipiikuni], 1911, Collection of Glenbow Library

Page 12: The Tipi Liners, Livingstone Range, southwestern Alberta, photograph by Anita Dammer © Glenbow Museum

Page 13 (top to bottom): Traditional Blackfoot Territory, map drawing by Rick Lalonde © Glenbow Museum; North Saskatchewan River, photograph by Anita Dammer © Glenbow Museum

Page 14 (top to bottom): Writing-On-Stone Provincial Park [Áísínai'pi], photograph by Anita Dammer © Glenbow Museum; The Great Sand Hill, photograph by Anita Dammer © Glenbow Museum

Chapter 2, Main Image: Writing-On-Stone Provincial Park [Áísínai'pi], photograph by Anita Dammer © Glenbow Museum; Inset: Tipi Pegs, Siksika, mid 20th century, black birch, Collection of Glenbow Museum

Page 16: Big Rock in Okotoks, photograph by Anita Dammer © Glenbow Museum

Page 17: Woman's Buffalo Jump, southwestern Alberta, photograph by Anita Dammer © Glenbow Museum

Page 18: Tipi Pegs, Siksika, mid 20th century, black birch, Collection of Glenbow Museum

Page 20–21: Edward S. Curtis, Peigan [Amsskaapipiikuni] Men Inside Lodge, 1910, Collection of Glenbow Archives, NA-1700-38

Page 24 (left to right): Robert Nathaniel Wilson, Antelope Tipi, Kainai Reserve, Alberta, 1892, Collection of Glenbow Archives, NA-668-8; Photographer Unknown, Bear Tipi, Blackfoot [Siksika] at Calgary Exhibition and Stampede Groups, Alberta, ca. 1920s, Collection of Glenbow Archives, NA-877-1

Page 25 (left to right): Robert Nathaniel Wilson, Star Tipi, Kainai Reserve, Alberta, 1892, Collection of Glenbow Archives, NA-668-10; Edward S. Curtis, Peigan [Amsskaaapiikuni] Painted Lodges [detail], 1900, Collection of Glenbow Archives, NA-1700-141

Page 26: Otter Flag Tipi, Niisitapiisinni: Our Way of Life, The Blackfoot Gallery, Siksika, mid 20th century, canvas, commercial paint, cotton thread, Collection of Glenbow Museum, photograph by Owen Melenka © Glenbow Museum

Chapter 3, Main Image: Edward S. Curtis, At the Water's Edge, Piegan [Amsskaapipiikuni], 1910, Collection of Glenbow Library; Inset: Shirt, Siksika, late 19th century, hide, porcupine quills, hawk bells, hair tin cones, feathers, glass beads, pigment, Collection of Glenbow Museum, AF 83

Page 28: Philip H. Godsell, One Gun, Blackfoot [Siksika], in Traditional Regalia, ca. 1930s, Collection of Glenbow Archives, NB-40-651

Page 29: Philip H. Godsell, Rides at the Door, Amsskaapipiikuni, 1951, Collection of Glenbow Archives, NB-40-842

Page 30 (top to bottom): Philip H. Godsell, Margaret Bad Boy, Siksika, Inside Tipi at The Calgary Stampede, Alberta, ca. 1940s, Collection of Glenbow Archives, NB-40-786; Photographer Unknown, Brings Down the Sun, Apatohsipiikuni, 1907, Archives of Manitoba, Morris, Edmund, NI 13566

Page 31 (top to bottom): Photographer Unknown, Decorated Tipis of Blackfoot, ca. 1900-03, Collection of Glenbow Archives, NA-919-37; Photographer Unknown, Peigan [Amsskaapiikuni] Encampment, Montana, ca. 1890s, Collection of Glenbow Archives, NA-1463-1; Royal Engineers, Blackfoot [Siksika] Indian Camp on the Prairies, Alberta, 1874, Collection of Glenbow Archives, NA-249-78

Page 32: Robert Nathaniel Wilson, Blood [Kainai] Camp, Southern Alberta, 1893, Collection of Glenbow Archives, NA-668-3

Page 33 (top to bottom): Edward S. Curtis, The Piegan

[Amsskaapipiikuni], 1910, Collection of Glenbow Library; Edward S. Curtis, **Three Peigan [Amsskaapipiikuni] Chiefs**, 1900, Collection of Glenbow Archives, NA-1700-139

Pages 34–35 (left to right): H.W.G. Stocken, **Blackfoot [Siksika] Women, Smoking Meat**, ca. early 1900s, Collection of Glenbow Archives, NA-3322-22; Photographer Unknown, **Blood [Kainai] Woman Drying Meat**, ca. 1920s, Collection of Glenbow Archives, NA-879-5; Photographer Unknown, **Camp of Peigan [Amsskaapiikuni]**, Montana, ca. 1890s, Collection of Glenbow Archives, NA-1463-51

Page 36 (top to bottom): Reiss T., **Blood [Kainai] Campsite**, 1931, Collection of Glenbow Archives, NA-5425-137; **Fleshing a Hide** [detail], Siksika, 1926, Collection of Glenbow Library

Page 37: Photographer Unknown, **Blood [Kainai] Woman**, Southern Alberta, 1904, Collection of Glenbow Archives, NA-2313-16

Page 38: **Shirt**, Siksika, late 19th century, hide, porcupine quills, hawk bells, hair tin cones, feathers, glass beads, pigment, Collection of Glenbow Museum, AF 83

Page 39 (top to bottom): **Shirt**, Siksika, late 19th century, hide, beads, stroud, weasel skin, feathers, wool, Collection of Glenbow Museum, AF 3460; **Dress**, Siksika, ca. 1910, buckskin, glass, cloth, sinew, Collection of Glenbow Museum, AF 1257

Page 40 (left to right): Reiss T., **Two Blackfeet [Amsskaapiikuni] Girls** [detail], ca. 1930s, Collection of Glenbow Archives, NA-5425-53; Photographer Unknown, **Blackfoot Woman and Child, Blackfoot [Siksika] Reserve**, Gleichen, Alberta, 1940, Collection of Glenbow Archives, NA-3092-94

Page 41: Edward S. Curtis, **Child's Lodge, Peigan [Amsskaapipiikuni]**, 1910, Collection of Glenbow Archives, NA-1700-35

Page 42: **Dolls**, Kainai, early 1900s, hide, glass beads, cotton, hair, feathers, metal, sinew, wood, Collection of Glenbow Museum, AF 4859 a-b

Page 43 (left to right): **Snake Pouch**, Siksika, early 20th century, Collection of Glenbow Museum, AF 370; **Lizard Pouch**, Apatohsipiikuni, early 20th century, Collection of Glenbow Museum, AF 4684

Page 44 (top to bottom): Edward S. Curtis, **Bringing the Sweat-Lodge Willows, Piegan [Amsskaapiikuni]**, 1900, Collection of Glenbow Library; Edward S. Curtis, **Piegan [Amsskaapiipikuni] Encampment**, 1900, Collection of Glenbow Library

Page 45: Photographer Unknown, **Platform Party at Chicken Dance, Blackfoot [Siksika] Reserve**, Southern Alberta, ca. 1930-35, Collection of Glenbow Archives, NA-4716-14

Page 46 (clockwise from top left): Photographer Unknown, **Christmas Dance on Blackfoot [Siksika] Reserve, Gleichen, Alberta**, ca. 1947, Collection of Glenbow Museum, NA-4440-3; Photographer Unknown, **Blackfoot [Siksika] Hospital near Gleichen, Alberta**, ca. 1930s, Collection of Glenbow Archives, NA-2966-12; Photographer Unknown, **Hand Game Played by Bloods [Kainai], Sarcee [Tsuu T'ina] Reserve, Alberta**, ca. 1960s, Collection of Glenbow Archives, NA-4897-10

Page 47 (left to right): Photographer Unknown, **Blackfoot [Siksika] Dancer in Full Regalia at Cluny, Alberta**, August 28, 1967, Collection of Glenbow Archives, NA-2557-87; **Blackfoot [Siksika] in Full Regalia, Dancing at Cluny, Alberta**, August 28, 1967, Collection of Glenbow Archives, NA-2557-80; **Blackfoot [Siksika] Boy Dancing at Cluny, Alberta**, August 28, 1967, Collection of Glenbow Archives, NA-2557-85

Page 48: Winold Reiss, **Double Steel and Two Cutter**, Amsskaapipiikuni, no date, pastel, charcoal, gouache on cardboard, Collection of Glenbow Museum, Gift of Mr. Louis W. Hill, St. Paul, Minnesota, 79.2.1

Page 49 (clockwise, from top left): Winold Reiss, **Big Bull**, Apatohsipiikuni, no date, pastel on paper, Collection of Glenbow Museum, Gift of the Devonian Foundation, R559.2; Reiss T., **Good Stealing Woman, Blackfeet [Amsskaapiikuni]**, ca. 1930s, Collection of Glenbow Archives, NA-5425-43; T.J. Hileman, **Weasel Tail**, Amsskaapiikuni, 1927, Collection of Glenbow Archives, NB-21-38; T.J. Hileman, **Eagle Arrow**, Kainai, 1927, Collection of Glenbow Archives, NB-21-4

Page 50 (left to right): Reiss T., **Mountain Chief (1848-1942), Blackfeet [Amsskaapiikuni]**, ca. 1930s, Collection of Glenbow Archives, NA-5425-58; Edward S. Curtis, **Old Person, Piegan [Amskaapiikuni]**, 1911, Collection of Glenbow Library

Chapter 4, Main Image: **Writing-On-Stone Provincial Park [Áísínai'pi]**, photograph by Anita Dammer © Glenbow Museum; Inset: Frederick Arthur Verner, **The Stampede** [detail], 1883, oil on canvas, Collection of Glenbow Museum, Purchased, 55.28

Page 52: Edward S. Curtis, **Blackfoot [Siksika] and Horse Travois**, 1926, Collection of Glenbow Archives, NA-1700-156; Sydney P. Hall, **Blackfoot [Siksika] People Crossing a River** [from "Canadian Pictures, Drawn with Pen and Pencil" by Marquess of Lorne, published in 1892], ca. 1881, Collection of Glenbow Archives, NA-843-2

Page 53: **One Year's Journey of a Amsskaapiikuni Family Through Northern Montana and Southern Alberta**, map drawing by Rick Lalonde © Glenbow Museum

Page 55: Edward S. Curtis, **Blackfoot [Siksika] Tipis**, 1926, Collection of Glenbow Archives, NA-1700-155

Page 56: Boorne and May, **Blood [Kainai] Women with Travois Breaking Camp on Belly River**, Alberta, 1887, Collection of Glenbow Archives, NA-250-2

Page 57 (top to bottom): Frederick Arthur Verner, **The Stampede**, 1883, oil on canvas, Collection of Glenbow Museum, Purchased, 1955, 55.28; William Jacob Hays, **The Stampede**, 1862, oil on canvas, Collection of Glenbow Museum, Purchased, 57.27

Page 58–59: **Head-Smashed-In Buffalo Jump**, southwestern Alberta, photograph by Anita Dammer © Glenbow Museum

Page 60: © Shutterstock.com / IPK Photography

Page 62: **Some Blackfoot Sacred Places in Southern Alberta and Northern Montana**, map drawing by Rick Lalonde © Glenbow Museum

Page 63: **Ninastako**, northwestern Montana, photograph by

Anita Dammer © Glenbow Museum

Page 64: Writing-On-Stone Provincial Park [Áísínai'pi], photograph by Anita Dammer © Glenbow Museum

Chapter 5, Main Image: Philip H. Godsell, Blackfoot with Travois in Regalia on Horseback During Calgary Stampede [detail], Alberta, ca. 1930s, Collection of Glenbow Archives, NB-40-757; Inset: Blackfoot Artifacts, late 19th to mid 20th century, Collection of Glenbow Museum

Page 67: Edward Whymper, Fort Edmonton, Alberta [from "Canadian Pictures, Drawn with Pen and Pencil" by Marquess of Lorne, published in 1892], ca. 1881, Collection of Glenbow Archives, NA-843-8

Page 68: Fur Trade Posts in Blackfoot Territory, map drawing by Rick Lalonde © Glenbow Museum

Page 69: Blackfoot Artifacts, late 19th to mid 20th century, Collection of Glenbow Museum

Page 70 (top to bottom): Bull Plume, Ledger Drawings, Apatohsipiikuni, early 20th century, Collection of Glenbow Archives, MH 188; Bull Plume, Ledger Drawings, Apatohsipiikuni, early 20th century, Collection of Glenbow Archives, MH 188; Bull Plume, Ledger Drawings, Apatohsipiikuni, early 20th century, Collection of Glenbow Archives, , MH 188

Page 71: Whisky Trade Posts in Northern Montana and Southern Alberta, map drawing by Rick Lalonde © Glenbow Museum

Page 72: Bull Plume, Ledger Drawings, Apatohsipiikuni, early 20th century, Collection of Glenbow Archives, MH 188

Page 73: Richard Barrington Nevitt, First Whiskey Spilled, 1874, watercolour and pencil on paper, Collection of Glenbow Museum, Purchased, 74.7.11

Page 74–75 (left to right): Gustavus Sohon, Sketch of Red Old Man, Peigan [Amsskaapipiikuni] Chief, October 9, 1855, Collection of Glenbow Archives, NA-360-1; Gustavus Sohon, White Bull or White Calf Bull, South Peigan [Ammsskaapipiikuni] Chief, October 9, 1855, Collection of Glenbow Archives, NA-360-12; Gustavus Sohon, Sketch of Lame Bull or Only Chief, Peigan [Amsskaapipiikuni] Chief, October 8, 1855, Collection of Glenbow Archives, NA-360-6

Page 76: Richard Barrington Nevitt, N.W.M.P Camp, Treaty #7, 1877, watercolour and pencil on paper, Collection of Glenbow Museum, Purchased with a grant from the Government of Alberta to mark the Alberta – RCMP Century Celebrations, 74.7.76

Chapter 6, Main Image: Woman's Buffalo Jump, southwestern Alberta, photograph by Anita Dammer © Glenbow Museum; Inset: Edward S. Curtis, The Blackfoot Country [detail], 1910, Collection of Glenbow Library

Page 80: Photographer Unknown, Blackfoot [Siksika] Encampment, Possibly Alberta, no date, Collection of Glenbow Archives, NA-3627-41

Page 81: Reiss T., Blackfeet [Amsskaapipiikuni] Dwellings on Reserve, Montana, ca. 1933, Collection of Glenbow Archives, NA-5425-124

Page 82: Photographer Unknown, Blood [Kainai] Woman Waiting at the Ration House, Blood Reserve, 1897, Collection of Glenbow Archives, NA-943-42

Page 83: Topley Studio, Close View of Group of Blackfoot [Siksika], Mounted, During Royal Visit to Calgary, Alberta, September 1901, Collection of Glenbow Archives, NA-539-4

Page 84: Boorne and May, Frank Tried to Fly and George Left Hand, Blackfoot [Siksika], Sowing Seed by Hand, ca. 1880s, Collection of Glenbow Archives, NA-127-1

Page 85: Photographer Unknown, Threshing on the Blood [Kainai] Reserve, Southern Alberta, 1915, Collection of Glenbow Archives, NA-4429-6

Page 86: Photographer Unknown, Blackfoot [Siksika] North Camp Boarding School Staff and Children, Gleichen Area, Alberta, 1890, Collection of Glenbow Archives, NA-1773-7

Page 87: Photographer Unknown, Peigan [Apatohsipiikuni] Children at Anglican Mission Picking Potatoes, Peigan Reserve, Alberta, ca. 1900, Collection of Glenbow Archives, NA-1020-25

Page 88 (top to bottom): Photographer Unknown, Girls' Dormitory, Old Sun School, Blackfoot [Siksika] Reserve, ca. 1955-57, Collection of Glenbow Archives, NA-4817-22; Clarke, Interior of St. Paul's Anglican School, Blood [Kainai] Reserve, Southern Alberta, ca. 1927, Collection of Glenbow Archives, NA-1811-55

Page 89: Present Blackfoot Reserves in Canada and the United States, map drawing by Rick Lalonde © Glenbow Museum

Page 91: Marcell, First Nations at First Calgary Exhibition and Stampede, Alberta, September 1912, Collection of Glenbow Archives, NA-274-3

Page 92–93: Philip H. Godsell, One Gun, Blackfoot [Siksika], in Regalia on Horseback at Calgary Stampede, Alberta, ca. 1940s, Collection of Glenbow Archives, NB-40-729

Page 94: Philip H. Godsell, Interior of Blackfoot [Siksika] Tipi at Calgary Stampede, Alberta, ca. 1940s, Collection of Glenbow Archives, NB-40-774

Chapter 7, Main Image: Edward S. Curtis, An Idle Hour, Piegan [Amsskaapipiikuni], 1910, Collection of Glenbow Library; Inset: Photographer Unknown, Weasel Calf and Wife, Siksika North Camp, July 15, 1907, Archives of Manitoba, Morris, Edmund 88, NI 13699

The Edward S. Curtis images used in this publication, along with more of his photographs, can be found in the following publications.

Curtis, Edward S. *The North American Indian, being a series of volumes picturing and describing the Indians of the United States and Alaska.* New York: Johnson Reprint Corp., 1970.

Curtis, Edward S. *The North American Indian, being a series of volumes picturing and describing the Indians of the United States and Alaska.* Seattle, Wash.: E.S. Curtis, 1907–1930.

Index

103